SWITZERLAND TRAVEL GUIDE 2024

YOUR EASY MANUAL TO SWISS BEAUTY, CULTURE, AND ADVENTURE WITH PRACTICAL TIPS AND UNMISSABLE HIGHLIGHTS

HELENA WEISS

Helena Weiss

CONTENTS

Introduction   vi
Switzerland   viii

1. PLANNING YOUR TRIP   1
   Best Time to Visit   1
   Travel Documents and Visas   2
   Currency and Budgeting   3
   Language preview   3
   Transportation   4
   Packing List   5
   Cultural Etiquette   6

2. ZURICH   7
   Attractions   8
   Best Places to Eat   10
   Where to Stay   11
   Day Trips   13

3. GENEVA   15
   Top Attractions   16
   Best Places to Eat   18
   Where to Stay   20
   Day Trips   22

4. BERN   24
   Top Attractions   25
   Places to Eat   27
   Where to stay   29
   Day Trips   31

5. BASEL   33
   Top Attractions   34
   Best Places to Eat   35
   Where to Stay   37
   Day Trips   38

6. LUCERNE   41
   Top Attractions   42
   Best Places to Eat   43

Where to Stay   44
Day Trips   45

7. LAUSANNE   47
Top Attractions in Lausanne   48
Best Places to Eat   49
Where to Stay   50
Day Trips   51

8. INTERLAKEN   54
Attractions   55
Places to Eat   56
Where to Stay   58
Outdoor Activities   60

9. ZERMATT   63
Attractions   64
Places to Eat   66
Where to Stay   68
Outdoor Activities   69

10. ST. MORITZ   73
Attractions   74
Places to Eat   75
Where to Stay   76
Winter Sports   78

11. LUGANO   81
Attractions   82
Places to Eat   83
Where to Stay   84
Day Trips   86

12. EXPERIENCES IN SWITZERLAND   88
Scenic Train Rides   88
Swiss Festivals and Events   90
Traditional Swiss Cuisine   92
Swiss Chocolate and Cheese Tours   93
Hiking and Nature Trails   94
Ski Resorts and Winter Activities   95
Practical Information recap   97

end   99

INTRODUCTION

Thank you for choosing this guide. **I've put in a lot of effort, sharing my experiences and gathering extra information to make it as complete as possible.** If you find any issues, please let me know.

Switzerland is a small, diverse country known for its beautiful landscapes, precision craftsmanship, and rich culture. People here are friendly and often speak multiple languages, including German, French, Italian, and English, making it easier for you to travel around.

It became a neutral state in 1815 and has not been involved in a foreign war since. This neutrality has made it a hub for international diplomacy and organizations. **You'll love the breathtaking scenery.** The Alps are majestic, the lakes are pristine, and the villages are charming. **Tourists come here for the world-class skiing resorts, picturesque hiking trails, and historical sites.** Most visitors come in winter for skiing and snowboarding, or in summer for hiking and exploring the outdoors.

The country is famous for its neutrality, banking system, high-quality watches, and delicious chocolate. **Swiss banks are known worldwide for their stability and security.** Swiss watches are famous for their precision and luxury, and the chocolate here is celebrated for its quality and taste. **Switzerland also produces fine cheeses, exceptional wines, and high-tech products.** The country's industries include pharmaceuticals, machinery, and financial services, contributing significantly to the global economy.

Switzerland has a big influence on the world. Its political neutrality and humanitarian efforts make it a hub for international organizations like the United Nations and the International Red Cross. The country's strong focus on education and research leads to many innovations, especially in science and technology.

You'll find that Switzerland is just as beautiful and well-organized as it looks online. It's really a nice place to visit almost one time. **Despite its small size of about 41,290 square kilometers, its global impact is huge, from its political stance to its contributions to culture and innovation.**

Thank you again for using this guide. **I hope it helps you make the most of your trip.** Let's see the Switzerland chapter.

SWITZERLAND

Before starting, now you are in a place where huge mountains touch the sky and clear lakes sparkle in the sun. This is what it's like here. The mountains are perfect for skiing in the winter and hiking in the summer. The base of the Matterhorn, a mountain that looks like it came from a fairy tale. Or maybe you take a train ride through the Alps, seeing amazing views from your window.

The lakes are just as beautiful. Lake Geneva is big and beautiful. You can sail on it, swim in it, or just sit by it and relax. There are castles like Château de Chillon right on its shores. Lake Lucerne is surrounded by mountains and has lovely boat trips. When you have free time, you can swim in the lake or just enjoy the beautiful view.

The cities are full of life and things to do. Zurich is a big city with a lot of shops and museums. You can walk down Bahnhofstrasse, which has some of the best shopping in the world. Then you can visit the old part of the city, which has narrow streets and old buildings. The Swiss National Museum is a great place to learn about the country's history.

Geneva is known for its international vibe. You can visit the United Nations and learn about global issues at the Red Cross Museum. The parks along Lake Geneva are perfect for a walk or a picnic. The Jet d'Eau fountain shoots water high into the air and is a must-see.

Bern, the capital, has a very old and charming feel. The medieval old town has beautiful old buildings and arcades. The Zytglogge clock tower has a little show every hour with moving figures. The Bear Park is a fun place to see bears up close.

Basel is at the meeting point of three countries: Switzerland, France, and

Germany. It has a big art scene with many museums like the Fondation Beyeler and the Kunstmuseum. Art Basel is a huge art fair that happens every year and draws people from all over the world.

Lausanne sits on the shores of Lake Geneva and is surrounded by vineyards. The Olympic Museum is here, and it has interesting exhibits about the history of the Olympic Games. The old town is charming with its Gothic cathedral and lively markets.

Interlaken is between two lakes, Lake Thun and Lake Brienz, and is known for adventure. You can take a train to Jungfraujoch, the highest railway station in Europe, for stunning views. Or you can go paragliding over the lakes for an unforgettable experience.

Zermatt is at the foot of the Matterhorn and is car-free, so it feels very peaceful. You can take a train up to Gornergrat for some of the best views in the Alps. In winter, you can ski all year round at the Matterhorn Glacier Paradise.

St. Moritz is famous for its luxury and winter sports. The frozen lake hosts polo matches and horse races in winter, making it a glamorous place to visit.

Lugano is in the Italian-speaking part of the country and has a warm, Mediterranean feel. There are palm trees and lakeside promenades. You can hike up Monte Brè for great views or enjoy the local culture in the town's squares and cafes.

2024

In 2024, there are many great reasons to visit. First, let's talk about the Montreux Jazz Festival. This famous festival happens every July by Lake Geneva. For two weeks, you can listen to the best musicians playing jazz, blues, rock, and pop. Imagine enjoying amazing music with the beautiful lake and mountains all around you.

In December, Geneva hosts the Fête de l'Escalade. This lively festival celebrates a big event from 1602 when the people of Geneva saved their city. The streets are full of parades, people in old costumes, and delicious chocolate cauldrons that you can taste.

In August, Zurich has the Street Parade. This is one of the biggest techno parties in the world. Picture the streets filled with colorful floats, loud music, and thousands of people dancing and having fun together. It's a huge, exciting party that shows Zurich's lively spirit.

If you love movies, go to Locarno in August for the Locarno Film Festival. This event has been happening since 1946. You can watch movies under the stars in the beautiful Piazza Grande, surrounded by the old town's charm.

For ski lovers, the Lauberhorn Ski Races in Wengen in January are a must-see. These races are part of the World Cup and have tough downhill and slalom courses. The stunning mountains like Eiger, Mönch, and Jungfrau make it even more exciting. The cheering fans and festive vibe make it an event to remember.

Art Basel in June is perfect for art fans. This top art fair brings galleries from all over the world. You can see amazing contemporary and modern art. Whether you're a serious art collector or just love looking at art, Art Basel is a fantastic event.

Swiss National Day on August 1st is a big celebration. Imagine watching spectacular fireworks, listening to traditional music, dancing, and enjoying bonfires. It's a day when everyone comes together to celebrate, and you can join in the fun.

In November, the Lausanne Lumières Festival lights up the city. Artists create beautiful light displays that make the streets and buildings look magical. Walking through the city, you will feel the festive and enchanting atmosphere.

If you love flowers, visit Morges in April for the Flower Festival. The town is covered with thousands of tulips. It's a bright and colorful way to celebrate spring and enjoy the beauty of the region.

FIRST TIME

I guess is your first time so, here are some nice things to know to make your vacation awesome.

Language: There are four official languages: German, French, Italian, and Romansh. Most people speak German in the central and eastern parts, French in the west, Italian in the south, and Romansh in a small part of the southeast. But don't worry, English is widely understood, especially in tourist areas and big cities, so you should be fine.

Money: The currency is the Swiss Franc (CHF). Credit and debit cards are widely accepted, but it's smart to carry some cash for small purchases or in rural areas. You can easily find ATMs in cities and towns.

Transport: Public transport is excellent. Trains, buses, and boats are clean, on time, and connect the whole country. Get a Swiss Travel Pass for unlimited travel on public transport and free or discounted entry to many museums and attractions. It's a good deal if you plan to travel a lot.

Etiquette: People are polite and reserved. Greet people with a handshake and make eye contact. In stores or restaurants, say "Grüezi" (hello in Swiss German), "Bonjour" (in French), or "Buongiorno" (in Italian). Being on time is important, so try to be punctual.

Dining: In restaurants, wait for the host to show you to a table. Tipping is not required since a service charge is included in the bill, but it's nice to leave a small tip if the service is good, about 5-10%.

Safety: It is very safe with low crime rates. Just stay aware of your surroundings and keep an eye on your belongings, especially in crowded areas.

Nature: If you plan to hike or ski, always check the weather and follow local advice. The mountains can be dangerous if you are not prepared. Stick to marked trails and tell someone your plans.

Health: Tap water is safe to drink and very good. Pharmacies are well-stocked and pharmacists can help with minor issues. It's a good idea to have travel insurance for any medical needs.

Shopping: Stores open from 9 AM to 6 PM, with shorter hours on Saturdays. Most are closed on Sundays, except in major train stations and tourist spots.

Electricity: The voltage is 230V, and the plugs are type J. You might need an adapter for your devices.

Cultural Insights: The country is very clean and orderly. Always throw away your trash properly and recycle if you can. Public displays of affection are minimal, and loud behavior is generally not appreciated.

CHAPTER 1
PLANNING YOUR TRIP

BEST TIME TO VISIT

S pring, from March to May, is a great time to visit. The weather warms up with temperatures from 8°C to 15°C. Flowers start to bloom, and the landscapes turn green. Hiking is wonderful now because the trails are clear and the views are beautiful. Visit the Flower Festival in Morges where thousands of tulips bloom along Lake Geneva.

Summer, from June to August, is the busiest time. The weather is warm, between 18°C and 28°C, perfect for outdoor activities. Swim in the lakes, hike in the mountains, and enjoy many festivals. The Montreux Jazz Festival in July is a big music event by Lake Geneva. The Locarno Film Festival in August features outdoor film screenings in Piazza Grande. Summer is also great for scenic train rides like the Glacier Express.

Autumn, from September to November, is quieter and cooler with temperatures from 8°C to 15°C. The leaves change color, creating beautiful landscapes. This is perfect for hiking and visiting vineyards, especially in the Lavaux region by Lake Geneva. Enjoy wine tastings and see the grape harvest. The Geneva International Film Festival in November is great for movie lovers.

Winter, from December to February, is ideal for skiing and snowboarding. The temperatures range from -2°C to 7°C. Ski resorts like Zermatt and St. Moritz are famous worldwide. Ski on well-groomed slopes and enjoy cozy mountain lodges. The Lauberhorn Ski Races in Wengen in January are exciting to watch. During winter, cities like Zurich and Basel have charming Christmas markets with festive lights and stalls selling gifts and warm drinks like mulled wine.

For skiing, come in winter from December to February. The slopes are perfect, and the atmosphere is magical. For hiking and outdoor activities, visit in spring or autumn, from March to May or September to November, when the weather is pleasant, and the trails are beautiful. If you love festivals and events, summer from June to August is the best time. Enjoy warm weather and vibrant festivals. If you prefer fewer crowds and stunning scenery, autumn from September to November is ideal with its colorful leaves and relaxed pace.

TRAVEL DOCUMENTS AND VISAS

First, check if you need a visa. If you are from the EU, USA, Canada, Australia, and many other countries, you do not need a visa for short stays up to 90 days. You can find this list on the embassy's website.

If you need a visa, you will need a valid passport. It should not be older than 10 years and must be valid for at least 3 months after your planned departure date. Fill out the visa application form from the embassy's website, print it, and sign it. You also need two recent passport-sized photos that meet the photo requirements.

You need to show proof of travel. This includes flight reservations or tickets. If you're staying with friends or family, get a letter of invitation from them. If you're staying in hotels, provide the hotel bookings for your whole stay.

You must show you have enough money to support yourself during your visit. Bank statements from the last three months, a letter from your employer confirming your job and salary, or proof of income if you're self-employed will work. The guideline is to have at least 100 CHF per day of your stay.

Travel insurance is necessary. You need insurance that covers medical expenses and emergencies, with coverage of at least 30,000 euros. Bring a copy of your insurance certificate.

There's a fee for the visa application, usually around 80 euros for adults and less for children. Check the exact fee on the embassy's website. Make an appointment at the nearest embassy or consulate. Arrive on time with all your documents. You might need to give fingerprints and have a short interview about your trip.

The visa processing time is usually about 15 days but can take longer during busy times. Apply at least a month before your travel date to be safe. Sometimes, it can take up to 30 days.

When you arrive, have your passport, visa (if needed), and supporting documents ready to show at the border. The officer might ask about your trip, so be ready to explain your plans clearly.

CURRENCY AND BUDGETING

The currency here is the Swiss Franc, shortened to CHF. You'll use coins and bills. Coins come in 5, 10, 20, and 50 Rappen, and 1, 2, and 5 Francs. Bills are in 10, 20, 50, 100, 200, and 1000 Francs.

Accommodation prices can be different. If you are on a budget, hostels or simple hotels cost around 80 to 120 CHF per night. Mid-range hotels, with more comfort, usually charge between 150 and 250 CHF per night. Luxury hotels start at 300 CHF per night and can go higher, especially in places like Zurich, Geneva, or St. Moritz.

Eating out also varies in cost. A meal at a budget restaurant costs about 20 to 30 CHF. At a mid-range restaurant, a three-course meal costs around 40 to 70 CHF. Fine dining can easily cost 100 CHF per person or more. To save money, you can eat breakfast and lunch at local bakeries or grocery stores.

Activities and attractions have different prices. Museum tickets usually cost between 10 and 20 CHF. Skiing for a day can cost 60 to 100 CHF, depending on the resort. Scenic train rides, like the Glacier Express, cost between 150 and 300 CHF for a round trip, depending on the class and route.

To manage your budget, plan ahead. Book your accommodations and activities early to get the best prices. Use public transport, which is very good and cheaper than renting a car. The Swiss Travel Pass lets you travel on trains, buses, and boats for a set number of days and gives free or discounted entry to many museums and attractions.

For meals, local bakeries or grocery stores are good for breakfast and lunch. For dinner, look for local places instead of tourist spots to save money.

When exchanging money, get some Swiss Francs before you arrive. Your home bank usually gives better rates than airport exchanges. Once here, use ATMs for cash; they give good rates, but check if your bank charges for international withdrawals. Credit and debit cards are widely accepted, but tell your bank you are traveling to avoid problems. Avoid exchange booths in tourist areas or airports because they have bad rates and high fees.

LANGUAGE PREVIEW

As i told you in the introduction chapter, In Switzerland you will hear four main languages: German, French, Italian, and Romansh. Most people speak German in the central and eastern parts, French in the west, and Italian in the south. Romansh is spoken in a small part of the southeast. While many people understand English, especially in tourist areas and big cities, knowing some simple phrases in the local languages will help a lot.

In German-speaking areas, say "Hallo" for hello, "Auf Wiedersehen" for goodbye, "Bitte" for please, "Danke" for thank you, "Ja" for yes, "Nein" for no, "Entschuldigung" for excuse me, "Sprechen Sie Englisch?" for do you speak English?, "Wie viel kostet das?" for how much does this cost?, and "Wo ist die Toilette?" for where is the bathroom.

In French-speaking areas, use "Bonjour" for hello, "Au revoir" for goodbye, "S'il vous plaît" for please, "Merci" for thank you, "Oui" for yes, "Non" for no, "Excusez-moi" for excuse me, "Parlez-vous anglais?" for do you speak English?, "Combien ça coûte?" for how much does this cost?, and "Où sont les toilettes?" for where is the bathroom.

In Italian-speaking areas, say "Ciao" or "Buongiorno" for hello, "Arrivederci" for goodbye, "Per favore" for please, "Grazie" for thank you, "Sì" for yes, "No" for no, "Mi scusi" for excuse me, "Parla inglese?" for do you speak English?, "Quanto costa?" for how much does this cost?, and "Dove sono i bagni?" for where is the bathroom.

Even though many people speak English, especially in tourist areas and big cities, knowing these basic phrases will help you get around and show respect for the swiss culture.

TRANSPORTATION

The main airports are in Zurich, Geneva, and Basel. From these airports, you can easily switch to trains, buses, or rental cars to reach your destination.

The train system is very good. Trains are clean and always on time. They connect cities, towns, and even small villages. Major routes include Zurich to Geneva, Zurich to Bern, and Zurich to Lucerne. You can book tickets in advance online through the SBB website or their app. Booking ahead is cheaper and ensures you have a seat. If you plan to travel a lot, get a Swiss Travel Pass. This pass gives you unlimited travel on trains, buses, and boats for a set number of days, plus free or discounted entry to many museums and attractions. For example, a 3-day pass costs around 232 CHF.

Renting a car gives you more freedom, especially if you want to explore rural areas or mountains. Major rental companies have offices at airports and in cities. Driving is easy, with clear road signs and good roads. Watch out for parking rules and fees, which can be high in cities. Park-and-ride options are a smart way to avoid city center traffic. In winter, make sure your rental car has winter tires and snow chains. Main routes include the A1, which runs east to west from

St. Gallen to Geneva, and the A2, which runs north to south from Basel to Chiasso.

Public transport in cities is very efficient. This includes buses, trams, and boats. You can buy tickets at machines, online, or with mobile apps. Cities like Zurich, Geneva, Basel, and Bern have frequent services that cover all major areas, making it easy to get around without a car. A single ticket in Zurich for a short trip costs around 2.70 CHF, while a day pass costs about 8.80 CHF. Day passes and multi-day tickets offer unlimited travel within the city for a set period, saving you money.

For long-distance trains, book tickets in advance through the SBB website or app for the best prices and guaranteed seats. The Swiss Travel Pass is perfect for tourists, offering unlimited travel on trains, buses, and boats, plus free museum entries. Use transport apps like SBB Mobile for train schedules, ticket bookings, and real-time updates. Local transport apps help you navigate city buses and trams. Major train stations have amenities like luggage storage, shops, and restaurants, with clear signs in multiple languages.

If you rent a car, learn the road rules. GPS helps with navigation, and planning your route avoids city center traffic where parking is tough. Always buy a ticket before boarding buses or trams. Ticket inspectors are common, and fines for traveling without a ticket are high.

Make sure to consider the time of year. In winter, check the weather forecast and road conditions if you are driving, as snow and ice can make travel difficult. Summer is peak tourist season, so book early. Spring and autumn offer mild weather and fewer crowds, making them ideal times to visit.

PACKING LIST

In spring, the weather changes a lot. Pack layers like long-sleeve shirts, t-shirts, and a lightweight sweater. Bring a waterproof jacket for rain. Comfortable pants or jeans are good for walking and hiking. You need waterproof hiking shoes or sturdy walking shoes to keep your feet dry. A small umbrella can be handy. Sunglasses and a hat will protect you on sunny days, and a scarf will keep you warm on cooler evenings.

Summer is warm, so pack light clothes like t-shirts, shorts, and dresses. Bring a swimsuit for lakes and pools. Evenings can be cool, especially in the mountains, so pack a light jacket or sweater. Comfortable walking shoes are a must for exploring cities, and sandals are great for warm days. If you plan to hike, bring hiking boots, a hat, and a small backpack. High SPF sunscreen is important to protect your skin from the strong sun.

In autumn, pack layers like long-sleeve shirts, sweaters, and t-shirts. A warm jacket is important for cooler days and evenings. Comfortable pants or jeans are perfect for daily wear. Waterproof hiking shoes or sturdy walking shoes are needed for exploring the autumn landscapes. Gloves, a scarf, and a hat will keep you warm on colder days. An umbrella will be useful for the occasional rain.

Winter needs warm clothing. Pack thermal underwear, sweaters, and long-sleeve shirts to stay warm. A heavy, waterproof winter coat is crucial. Insulated pants or jeans will keep your legs warm. Waterproof boots with good traction are a must for snow and ice. Don't forget warm gloves, a hat, and a scarf. Layering is key, so bring base layers, mid-layers, and outer layers. Also, pack a swimsuit because many hotels have indoor pools or saunas.

CULTURAL ETIQUETTE

When you greet someone, say "Grüezi" in German-speaking areas, "Bonjour" in French-speaking regions, or "Buongiorno" in Italian-speaking parts. If you are not sure, "Grüezi" works well. Shake hands with a smile and eye contact. Close friends might greet with three cheek kisses, starting on the right cheek. Be on time for everything. Keep a comfortable distance from people and avoid touching if you don't know them well.

In restaurants, wait for the host to seat you. Once seated, say "En Guete" before starting your meal, which means "Enjoy your meal." Keep your hands visible on the table, but don't rest your elbows on it. Use the fork in your left hand and the knife in your right, and don't switch hands. Finish all the food on your plate. Tipping isn't required since service is included, but rounding up the bill or leaving a small tip for good service is appreciated.

In public places, keep your voice down. As you may know already loud conversations are considered rude. Smoking is banned in many public places, including restaurants, bars, and public transport, so use designated smoking areas.

CHAPTER 2
ZURICH

Z urich is the biggest city and a key financial center. It has a rich history dating back to Roman times when it was called Turicum. The city is known for its old buildings and modern skyscrapers.

In the Old Town, you can see the Grossmünster and Fraumünster churches. The Grossmünster has twin towers and is a major landmark. The Fraumünster is famous for its stained glass windows by Marc Chagall.

Bahnhofstrasse is a main shopping street with luxury boutiques and global brands. It's one of the most exclusive shopping streets in the world.

The city has over 50 museums and 100 galleries. The Kunsthaus is a top spot for art lovers with works by Giacometti, Chagall, and Picasso. The Swiss National Museum looks like a fairy-tale castle and tells the story of the country's history and culture.

Located along Lake Zurich, the city offers beautiful natural views. You can enjoy boating, swimming, and cycling by the lake. In summer, lakeside parks are great for picnics and sunbathing. In winter, you can ice skate or ski in the nearby Alps.

You can try traditional Swiss dishes like fondue and raclette or enjoy international cuisine. There are cozy family-run restaurants and high-end dining spots that use local ingredients and Swiss culinary traditions.

Moving in the city is pretty easy with trams, buses, and trains. They are clean and always on time, making it simple to reach the places you want to see.

ATTRACTIONS

Lake Zurich is a beautiful spot where you can relax and enjoy nature. To get there, take tram number 4 or bus number 161 from the city center. The lake is close to downtown and easy to reach. You can take a boat ride, rent a paddle-board, or kayak to explore the water. In the summer, you can swim at Strandbad Mythenquai, which costs around 8 CHF for adults. It is open from 9 AM to 8 PM. Walking along the lakeside promenade is also lovely. Try a sunset cruise for an unforgettable experience, with prices starting at 25 CHF.

The Old Town, or Altstadt, is the historic heart of Zurich. You can reach it by tram numbers 4, 6, or 10, or simply walk from the city center. In the Old Town, visit the **Grossmünster church**, famous for its twin towers.

Climbing the towers costs 5 CHF and gives you amazing city views. The Fraumünster church is nearby, known for its beautiful stained glass windows by Marc Chagall. Walking through the narrow, winding streets, you'll find hidden courtyards and quaint shops. The Lindenhof park offers a peaceful place to relax with great views of the city and the river. The Old Town is free to explore, and many sites are open from 9 AM to 6 PM.

Bahnhofstrasse is one of the world's most exclusive shopping streets, running from the main train station to Lake Zurich. You can reach it easily by tram or walking from the city center. Here, you'll find luxury boutiques, Swiss watch stores, and upscale department stores. The street is beautifully decorated during the holiday season. Visit Confiserie Sprüngli for famous chocolates and pastries. Shopping on Bahnhofstrasse is an experience in itself, and window shopping is free, but prices in the stores can be very high. Most shops are open from 9 AM to 7 PM, Monday to Saturday.

The Swiss National Museum is located next to the main train station, in a building that looks like a castle. You can reach it by tram, bus, or a short walk from the city center. The museum covers Swiss history and culture, with exhibits ranging from prehistoric artifacts to modern art. Highlights include the medieval section with armor and weaponry and beautifully crafted furniture. Admission is 10 CHF for adults, and it is open from 10 AM to 5 PM, Tuesday to Sunday. Audio guides are available and provide detailed information about the exhibits. After your visit, relax at the museum's café.

For Lake Zurich, you have to wear comfortable shoes and bring a swimsuit if you plan to swim. It gets busy on weekends, so visit early or late to avoid crowds. In the Old Town, take your time to wander and discover hidden gems. A guided tour can offer more insights into the area's history. When you are visiting Bahnhofstrasse, be prepared for high prices. At the Swiss National Museum, check for special exhibitions or events when you are in Town.

BEST PLACES TO EAT

Kronenhalle is located at Rämistrasse 4, near Bellevue Square. To get there, take tram lines 2, 4, 5, 8, 9, or 11 to the Bellevue stop. Kronenhalle is known for its classic Swiss food and impressive art collection. Try the Zürcher Geschnetzeltes, a creamy veal dish with mushrooms, served with Rösti, which is a Swiss potato pancake. For dessert, have the chocolate mousse. Prices are high, with main dishes costing 40 to 60 CHF. It's popular with both locals and tourists, so make a reservation. The restaurant is open daily from 12 PM to 12 AM and is highly rated for its food and unique atmosphere.

Zeughauskeller is at Bahnhofstrasse 28a, housed in an old arsenal. You can get there by taking tram lines 6, 7, 10, 11, or 13 to the Paradeplatz stop. This place offers hearty Swiss food in a lively setting. Try the Zürcher Eintopf, a local stew, or the famous sausages with sauerkraut and potatoes. For dessert, get the Apfelstrudel with vanilla sauce. Main dishes cost 25 to 40 CHF. It's a great spot for both tourists and locals. Zeughauskeller is open daily from 11:30 AM to 11 PM and is well-rated for its traditional food and vibrant atmosphere.

Haus Hiltl is at Sihlstrasse 28. Take tram lines 2 or 9 to the Sihlstrasse stop. Haus Hiltl is the world's oldest vegetarian restaurant, open since 1898. The menu has many vegetarian and vegan dishes. Try the Hiltl Tartar, a vegan tartare. The buffet is also popular, with lots of salads, hot dishes, and desserts. For dessert, try the tiramisu. Prices are reasonable, around 20 to 30 CHF per plate. It's popular with both locals and tourists and is open from 6 AM to 11 PM on weekdays and 8 AM to 11 PM on weekends. It's highly rated for its vegetarian food.

Le Dézaley is located at Römergasse 7, near Grossmünster. Take tram lines 4 or 15 to the Helmhaus stop. This cozy restaurant specializes in fondue and other Swiss Alpine dishes. Try the cheese fondue or the Fondue Chinoise, a hot pot with thinly sliced meat. The raclette is also a favorite. For dessert, try the chocolate fondue. Main dishes cost 30 to 50 CHF. It's well-loved by both locals and tourists and is open daily from 11:30 AM to 11 PM. It's highly rated for its authentic food and warm atmosphere.

Restaurant Adler's Swiss Chuchi is at Rosengasse 10 in the Old Town. Take tram lines 4, 6, or 10 to the Rudolf-Brun-Brücke stop. This restaurant is known for its authentic Swiss dishes. Try the cheese fondue and raclette. The menu also has Älplermagronen, a Swiss macaroni and cheese with potatoes, onions, and applesauce. For dessert, try the Swiss chocolate cake. Main dishes cost 25 to 45 CHF. It's popular with tourists and locals and is open daily from 11:30 AM to 10 PM. It's highly rated for its traditional food and charming decor.

Seerose is at Seestrasse 493 on Lake Zurich. Take tram line 7 to the Wollishofen stop. Seerose offers Swiss and Mediterranean food with stunning lake views. On the terrace, enjoy dishes like grilled fish, fresh salads, and local wines. For dessert, try the panna cotta. Main dishes cost 40 to 70 CHF. It's a favorite for special occasions and romantic dinners. Seerose is open daily from 11:30 AM to 11 PM. Reservations are recommended, especially for outdoor seating. It's highly rated for its views and excellent food.

WHERE TO STAY

Old Town (Altstadt):
Hotel Adler
Hotel Adler is in the heart of the Old Town at Rosengasse 10. You can get there by taking tram lines 4, 6, or 10 to the Rudolf-Brun-Brücke stop. The hotel has cozy rooms with local art, free Wi-Fi, and a restaurant that serves Swiss food. Prices range from 150 to 250 CHF per night. You'll be close to Grossmünster and Bahnhofstrasse, making it easy to explore. This hotel is popular with tourists because of its great location.

Baur au Lac

Baur au Lac is at Talstrasse 1, near Lake Zurich and Bahnhofstrasse. Take tram lines 2 or 4 to the Bürkliplatz stop. The rooms are elegant and offer views of the lake or park. Prices start at 600 CHF per night. The hotel has fine dining, a fitness center, and a private garden. This luxury hotel is perfect for those who want a high-end experience and are close to shopping and dining.

Zurich West:

25hours Hotel Zurich West

25hours Hotel Zurich West is at Pfingstweidstrasse 102 in the Zurich West area. You can reach it by taking tram line 4 to the Toni-Areal stop. The hotel has a colorful, modern design and offers free bike rentals, a sauna, and a restaurant with international food. Prices range from 150 to 250 CHF per night. Zurich West is known for its nightlife, art galleries, and trendy restaurants, making it a good choice for young travelers or those looking for a lively area.

Budget Accommodation:

Youth Hostel Zurich

Youth Hostel Zurich is at Mutschellenstrasse 114, a 10-minute walk from Wollishofen train station. You can also take tram line 7 to the Morgental stop and walk from there. Prices range from 40 to 80 CHF per night for dorm beds or private rooms. The hostel has free Wi-Fi, breakfast, and a kitchen for guests. It's great for backpackers or budget travelers. Nearby Lake Zurich offers beautiful walking paths and easy access to public transport.

Mid Options:

Hotel Marta

Hotel Marta is at Zähringerstrasse 36, close to the main train station. You can get there by taking tram lines 4, 6, or 10 to the Central stop. The rooms are simple but comfortable, and prices range from 100 to 200 CHF per night. The hotel offers free Wi-Fi and breakfast. Its central location makes it easy to explore the Old Town and Bahnhofstrasse on foot.

Hotel St. Josef

Hotel St. Josef is at Hirschengraben 64, near ETH Zurich and the University of Zurich. You can reach it by taking tram lines 6, 9, or 10 to the ETH/Universitätsspital stop. The rooms are bright and spacious, with prices from 150 to 250 CHF per night. The hotel offers free Wi-Fi, breakfast, and a restaurant. It's a good choice for visitors who want a quiet stay close to cultural sites and schools.

Luxury Options:

The Dolder Grand

The Dolder Grand is on a hill at Kurhausstrasse 65, offering great views of the city and Lake Zurich. Take tram line 3 to the Römerhof stop and then the Dolder-bahn to the final stop. The rooms are luxurious, with prices starting at 700 CHF per night. The hotel has a world-class spa, fine dining, and a large art collection. It's perfect for a luxurious getaway with excellent services and amenities.

DAY TRIPS

Lucerne is a beautiful city about an hour away by train. Take a direct train from the main train station to Lucerne, which runs frequently and takes about 50 minutes. When you arrive, start your day by visiting the Chapel Bridge, a stunning wooden bridge with paintings and a historic tower. Explore the Old Town with its charming squares and the famous Lion Monument, a touching tribute to the Swiss Guards. Take a boat trip on Lake Lucerne for breathtaking views of the mountains. Don't miss the cable car ride up to Mount Pilatus for panoramic views and hiking. Trains to Lucerne cost around 25 CHF each way.

Rapperswil, also known as the "Town of Roses," is a picturesque town on the shores of Lake Zurich, about 40 minutes away by train or boat. Take a train from the main station or enjoy a scenic boat ride on Lake Zurich. Start with a stroll through the beautiful rose gardens, which bloom from May to October. Visit Rapperswil Castle for panoramic views of the lake. Walk across the wooden bridge to the nearby town of Hurden for a peaceful experience. Explore the charming streets of the Old Town, discover local museums, and enjoy the relaxed atmosphere. A train ticket costs about 15 CHF each way, and the boat ride is a bit more expensive but offers stunning views.

Rhine Falls, Europe's largest waterfall, is about an hour away by train. Take a direct train to Schaffhausen, and from there, a short bus ride to the falls. Get up close to the falls with a thrilling boat tour that takes you to the rock in the middle of the roaring waters. Walk along the viewing platforms for different perspectives. Visit Laufen Castle, which offers a unique view and historical insights. Enjoy the natural beauty and the power of the cascading water. The train ticket costs around 30 CHF each way, and the boat tour costs about 10 CHF.

Mount Titlis is a stunning mountain destination about two hours from Zurich. Take a train to Engelberg and then ride a series of cable cars to the summit. The rotating cable car to the top offers amazing views. Walk across the Titlis Cliff Walk, the highest suspension bridge in Europe. Explore the Glacier Cave, a magical world of ice, and enjoy snow activities like tubing or sledding. The train ticket costs around 50 CHF each way, and the cable car ride to the summit is about 90 CHF for a round trip.

Stein am Rhein is a charming medieval town about an hour and a half from Zurich by train. Take a train to Stein am Rhein, with one transfer along the way. Stroll through the beautifully preserved Old Town with its colorful frescoed buildings. Visit Hohenklingen Castle for panoramic views of the town and river. Explore local museums and enjoy a meal at a riverside restaurant, taking in the serene beauty of the area. The train ticket costs about 25 CHF each way.

CHAPTER 3
GENEVA

G eneva is a beautiful city on the shores of Lake Geneva, with the Alps as a stunning backdrop. Founded over two thousand years ago by the Romans, it has grown into a global hub for diplomacy and finance. It is home to the United Nations' European headquarters and the International Red Cross. This makes the city very important on the world stage.

The Old Town is full of history. Walking through its cobblestone streets, you will find St. Peter's Cathedral, a church from the 12th century. Climb its towers for amazing views of the city and lake. The Old Town is a place where every street and building has a story to tell.

One of the most famous landmarks is the **Jet d'Eau**, a huge fountain that shoots water 140 meters into the air. It looks especially beautiful at sunset. The lake is a central part of life in the city, offering boat cruises, paddleboarding, and lovely promenades for walking or picnicking.

The city has many museums. The Museum of Art and History is one of the largest, with collections from ancient to modern times. The Natural History Museum has interesting exhibits on plants and animals from around the world. If you love watches, visit the Patek Philippe Museum to see beautiful timepieces and learn about Swiss watchmaking.

Geneva hosts many events. The Geneva International Motor Show is a big event for car lovers, showing the latest in car design. In summer, the Fêtes de Genève brings fireworks, concerts, and parades, creating a festive atmosphere enjoyed by everyone.

For shopping, head to Rue du Rhône. This street is lined with luxury shops, famous watchmakers, and designer stores. It's perfect for shopping or just looking at the beautiful displays.

The food scene is diverse. You can find traditional Swiss dishes like fondue and raclette, as well as food from all over the world. The city's many restaurants reflect its multicultural population, so there's something for every taste.

Here in Geneva is pretty easy to visit with trams, buses, and boats. The city's location also makes it a great starting point for trips to nearby places. You can visit Montreux, a charming town known for its jazz festival, or Lausanne, a city with a rich history. The Jura Mountains are also close, offering beautiful scenery and outdoor activities.

TOP ATTRACTIONS

Jet d'Eau is one of the tallest fountains in the world, shooting water 140 meters into the air. It is located at the end of the pier on Lake Geneva, near the English Garden (Jardin Anglais). You can reach it by walking along the lake from the city center or taking tram lines 6, 8, 9, or 25 to the "Jardin Anglais" stop. The best time to visit is at sunset, when the light makes the water sparkle. The fountain operates daily from 10 AM to 11 PM, weather permitting, and is free to visit. Be prepared to get a bit wet if the wind shifts, as the spray can reach the pier.

St. Pierre Cathedral is in the Old Town (Vieille Ville) at Place du Bourg-de-Four 24.

You can get there by taking tram lines 12 or 18 to the "Molard" stop, then walking up the hill. Inside, you will find beautiful stained glass windows and ancient artifacts. For a small fee of 5 CHF, you can climb the towers to get one of the best views of the city and lake. The archaeological site beneath the cathedral, showcasing ruins from Roman times, costs an additional 8 CHF. The cathedral is open Monday to Saturday from 10 AM to 5:30 PM and Sunday from 12

PM to 5:30 PM. Check the opening hours for the archaeological site, as they may vary.

International Red Cross and Red Crescent Museum is located at Avenue de la Paix 17, near the United Nations Office. You can reach it by taking tram line 15 to the "Nations" stop and then walking for about 10 minutes. The museum tells the story of the Red Cross's work worldwide through interactive exhibits and real-life stories. The admission fee is 15 CHF for adults and 7 CHF for students and seniors. The museum is open Tuesday to Sunday from 10 AM to 5 PM and is closed on Mondays. Plan to spend a few hours here to fully explore the exhibits.

United Nations Office is located at Palais des Nations, Avenue de la Paix 14. You can get there by taking tram line 15 to the "Nations" stop. Guided tours are available in several languages and provide insights into the UN's work and access to important rooms like the Assembly Hall and the Council Chamber. Tours cost 15 CHF for adults and 13 CHF for students and seniors. Bring your passport for security checks. The grounds also feature a park with sculptures and a beautiful view of the lake, which you can enjoy before or after your tour. Tours are available Monday to Friday from 10 AM to 4 PM, with the last tour starting at 4 PM.

For the **Jet d'Eau**, visit at sunset for the best views. Wear a waterproof jacket if you plan to get close, as the wind can change direction quickly, and you might get sprayed. At **St. Pierre Cathedral**, climbing the towers is a must for the best views, and visiting the archaeological site offers a deep dive into history. Spend a few hours at the **International Red Cross and Red Crescent Museum** to fully appreciate the exhibits, and try to visit on a weekday to avoid crowds. When visiting the **United Nations Office**, book your tour in advance and bring your passport for security checks. Combining the UN tour with the nearby Red Cross Museum can make the most of your time.

BEST PLACES TO EAT

Les Armures is a historic restaurant located right in the heart of the Old Town at Rue du Puits-Saint-Pierre 1. You can get there by taking tram lines 12 or 18 to the "Molard" stop, then walking up the hill. The building dates back to the 17th century, which gives it a cozy and authentic Swiss atmosphere. When you dine here, you must try the **fondue**, a classic Swiss dish made from melted cheese, usually a mix of Gruyère and Emmental, served with bread cubes for dipping. Another favorite is the **raclette**, where melted cheese is scraped onto boiled pota-toes, pickles, and onions. For dessert, try the **meringues with double cream**. The restaurant is open daily from 12 PM to 2 PM for lunch and from 7 PM to 10 PM for dinner. Given its popularity, especially among tourists, it's wise to make a reservation, particularly on weekends. Prices for main courses range from 30 to 50 CHF.

Café du Soleil, located at Place du Petit-Saconnex 6, is one of the oldest restaurants in the city and is famous for its exceptional **cheese fondue**. To reach it, take bus line 3 to the "Petit-Saconnex" stop. The fondue here is made with a mix of Gruyère and Vacherin Fribourgeois cheeses, giving it a rich and creamy flavor that is unforgettable. The café also offers other Swiss specialties such as **rosti**, a Swiss-style hash brown, and **Geneva-style perch fillets**, which are fresh fish from Lake Geneva often served with a buttery sauce. Open daily from 12 PM to 11 PM, this restaurant has a warm and friendly atmosphere. Prices for main courses range from 20 to 40 CHF. It's a bit outside the city center but well worth the visit.

Bistrot du Bœuf Rouge at Rue Dr-Alfred-Vincent 17 is a cozy French bistro known for its excellent **steak dishes** and traditional French cuisine. You can get there by taking tram lines 15 or 17 to the "Butini" stop and then walking a short distance. The **steak frites**, featuring a perfectly cooked steak served with crispy fries, and the **entrecôte**, a tender rib-eye steak, are highly recommended. The bistro also offers a fine selection of French wines to complement your meal. For dessert, try the **tarte Tatin**, a delicious caramelized apple tart. Bistrot du Bœuf Rouge is open Monday to Friday from 12 PM to 2 PM and from 7 PM to 10 PM, and on Saturday from 7 PM to 10 PM. Prices for main courses range from 25 to 50 CHF. The intimate and charming atmosphere makes it a great choice for a romantic dinner or a special occasion.

La Bottega, situated at Rue de la Corraterie 21, is an Italian restaurant with a contemporary twist. To reach it, take tram lines 12 or 14 to the "Bel-Air" stop. The sleek, modern design of the restaurant is matched by its innovative menu, which features dishes made from fresh, high-quality ingredients. **Homemade pasta** and **creative seafood dishes** are standout options. For dessert, try the **tiramisu**, a classic Italian treat. Open Monday to Friday from 12 PM to 2 PM and from 7 PM to 10 PM, and on Saturday from 7 PM to 10 PM, La Bottega is very popular, so reservations are highly recommended. Prices for main courses range from 30 to 60 CHF.

Bayview by Michel Roth is located in the Hotel President Wilson at Quai Wilson 47. You can get there by taking tram line 15 to the "Nations" stop and walking along the lake. This Michelin-starred restaurant offers an exquisite dining experience with **French haute cuisine** that focuses on seasonal ingredients. The **tasting menu** is an excellent way to experience the chef's culinary mastery, with dishes that are both visually stunning and delicious. For dessert, indulge in the **chocolate soufflé**. Bayview is open Tuesday to Friday for lunch from 12 PM to 1:30 PM, and from Tuesday to Saturday for dinner from 7 PM to 9:30 PM. Prices for the tasting menu start at 120 CHF, making this restaurant perfect for special occasions or a luxurious dining experience.

Le Jardin, situated in the Hotel Richemond at Jardin Brunswick, offers a fine dining experience with a menu that emphasizes local and seasonal ingredients. To reach it, take tram lines 12 or 14 to the "Brunswick" stop. The restaurant serves **contemporary European cuisine with a Mediterranean influence**. During the summer, the outdoor terrace is particularly lovely. Try the **sea bass with fennel and orange** for a main course and the **lemon tart** for dessert. Le Jardin is open Monday to Friday from 12 PM to 2 PM and from 7 PM to 10 PM, and on Saturday from 7 PM to 10 PM. Prices for main courses range from 40 to 70 CHF. Reservations are recommended, especially for terrace seating.

And of course the local dishes. **Cheese fondue** is a must, a delicious blend of melted cheeses, typically Gruyère and Emmental, served with bread cubes for dipping. **Raclette** is another classic, with melted cheese served over boiled potatoes, pickles, and onions. For seafood lovers, **perch fillets** from Lake Geneva, usually served with a buttery sauce and potatoes, are a local delicacy. **Rösti**, a Swiss potato dish similar to hash browns, is often served as a side dish and pairs well with many main courses. **Longeole**, a traditional Geneva sausage made with pork and fennel seeds, typically served with boiled potatoes and lentils, offers a hearty and flavorful taste of local cuisine.

WHERE TO STAY

Hotel Les Armures is in the heart of the Old Town at Rue du Puits-Saint-Pierre 1. This historic hotel is perfect if you want to experience the charm of the 17th century with modern comforts. The rooms are elegant with antique furniture, free Wi-Fi, air conditioning, and minibars. You can get here by taking tram lines 12 or 18 to the "Molard" stop and walking up the hill. You'll be close to **St. Pierre Cathedral**, **Old Town's cobblestone streets**, and several museums. Prices start at **400 CHF per night**. This hotel is very popular with tourists who enjoy a blend of luxury and history.

Hotel Central at Rue de la Rôtisserie 2 is a good choice for budget travelers. The rooms are simple but clean, with free Wi-Fi and breakfast included. It's a short walk from the "Molard" tram stop. Staying here puts you near the **Jet d'Eau**, the **English Garden**, and many shops and restaurants. Prices start at **100 CHF per night**. It's perfect for those who want a central location without spending too much.

Hotel Beau-Rivage, located at Quai du Mont-Blanc 13, offers stunning views of Lake Geneva. The spacious, elegantly decorated rooms come with free Wi-Fi, a fitness center, and fine dining options. You can get here by taking tram lines 15 or 17 to the "Mont-Blanc" stop and enjoying a scenic walk along the lake. Nearby are the **Jet d'Eau**, the **Brunswick Monument**, and the **Paquis Baths**. Prices start at **600 CHF per night**. This hotel is popular among luxury travelers who appreciate top-notch service and beautiful views.

For a mid-range option, **Hotel Edelweiss** at Place de la Navigation 2 offers a charming Swiss chalet experience. The themed rooms, free Wi-Fi, and traditional Swiss restaurant with live folk music make it a unique choice. It's near the "Gare Cornavin" tram stop. Nearby attractions include the **Paquis Baths**, the **Botanical Gardens**, and many international restaurants. Prices start at **200 CHF per night**. This hotel is popular with families and tourists looking for a unique cultural experience.

Hotel President Wilson at Quai Wilson 47 provides an ultra-luxurious stay with panoramic views of Lake Geneva and the Alps. The hotel features a spa, a heated outdoor pool, and several restaurants, including the Michelin-starred Bayview by Michel Roth. It's accessible via tram line 15 to the "Nations" stop and a pleasant walk along the lake. Nearby are the **United Nations Office**, the **International Red Cross and Red Crescent Museum**, and **Parc La Grange**. Prices start at **700 CHF per night**. This hotel is favored by business travelers and luxury seekers.

Hotel Sagitta at Rue de la Flèche 6 is a budget-friendly choice in Eaux-Vives. It offers comfortable rooms with kitchenettes, free Wi-Fi, and breakfast included. It's close to the "Terrassière" tram stop. Nearby, you'll find the **Jet d'Eau**, **Parc des Eaux-Vives**, and many shops and cafes. Prices start at **150 CHF per night**. This hotel is popular with families and long-term travelers.

Hotel Tiffany at Rue de l'Arquebuse 20 offers a boutique experience with Art Nouveau décor. The elegant rooms, wellness area, and on-site restaurant serving French cuisine create a stylish stay. It's near the "Plainpalais" tram stop. Nearby attractions include the **Plainpalais Flea Market**, the **Museum of Art and History**, and lively nightlife. Prices start at **250 CHF per night**. This hotel is popular with couples and cultural enthusiasts.

ibis Genève Centre Plainpalais at Rue de Carouge 15 is a modern, affordable option. The rooms are clean, with free Wi-Fi and breakfast available. It's close to the "Pont-d'Arve" tram stop. Nearby, you'll find the **Plainpalais Flea Market**, the **University of Geneva**, and many bars and restaurants. Prices start at **120 CHF per night**. This hotel is popular with budget travelers and students.

DAY TRIPS

Montreux:

Montreux is just an hour away by train. Go to the main station (Cornavin) and take a direct train. A return ticket costs about **50 CHF**. When you arrive, walk along the **Montreux Lakeside Promenade**. The views of the lake and Alps are amazing. The promenade has beautiful gardens, statues, and artwork.

Visit **Chillon Castle**, a medieval fortress on a small island in Lake Geneva. It is open from 9 AM to 7 PM in summer and 10 AM to 5 PM in winter. Entry costs **12.50 CHF**. Explore the castle's rooms, dungeons, and towers, and learn about its history with detailed exhibits and guided tours. For lunch, find a café in Montreux's old town. If you visit in July, the **Montreux Jazz Festival** is a must-see.

Take the 9 AM train from Geneva to Montreux. Arrive around 10 AM, walk along the lakeside, visit Chillon Castle, have lunch in the old town, and return to Geneva by an early evening train.

Gruyères:

Gruyères is about two hours away by train. Take a train from Geneva to Montreux, then switch to a regional train to Gruyères. A round trip is about **60 CHF**. Visit **Gruyères Castle**. It is open from 9 AM to 6 PM in summer and 10 AM to 5 PM in winter. Entry costs **12 CHF**. Enjoy panoramic views and explore the castle's rooms and gardens. For lunch, try a local restaurant in the town square and taste the famous **Gruyère cheese**. Visit the **HR Giger Museum**, dedicated to the artist known for his work on the "Alien" movie series. Entry costs **12.50 CHF**. In the afternoon, go to the **Maison Cailler chocolate factory** in nearby Broc. The factory offers tours with tastings. It is open from 10 AM to 5 PM, and the tour costs **12 CHF**.

Take an early train from Geneva to Montreux, transfer to Gruyères, visit Gruyères Castle, enjoy lunch, explore the HR Giger Museum, and tour the Maison Cailler chocolate factory before returning to Geneva by early evening.

Annecy, France:

Annecy, the "Venice of the Alps," is about an hour away by bus from Geneva. Buses leave from Gare Routière, Geneva's main bus station. A round trip costs about **20 EUR**. When you arrive, stroll through Annecy's old town, where canals weave through medieval buildings and colorful houses. Visit the **Château d'Annecy**, a restored castle with stunning views of the town and lake. It is open from 10:30 AM to 6 PM, and entry costs **5.50 EUR**. For lunch, dine at one of the many restaurants along the canals, enjoying local French cuisine. After lunch, take a boat cruise on **Lake Annecy** to enjoy the beautiful scenery from the water.

Cruises are available throughout the day and cost around **15 EUR** for a one-hour tour.

Take a bus from Geneva to Annecy, explore the old town, visit Château d'Annecy, have lunch by the canals, take a boat cruise on Lake Annecy, and return to Geneva by early evening bus.

Lausanne:

Lausanne is about 40 minutes away by train from Geneva. A return ticket costs around **25 CHF**. Start your day at the **Olympic Museum**, which has fascinating exhibits on the history of the Olympic Games. It is open from 9 AM to 6 PM, and entry costs **18 CHF**. Spend a few hours exploring the exhibits. Next, go to **Lausanne Cathedral**, a stunning Gothic building in the old town. It is open from 9 AM to 5:30 PM. Climb the tower for panoramic views of the city and lake. For lunch, choose a lakeside restaurant in the **Ouchy area** and try the local specialty, **perch fillets**. After lunch, take a walk along the Ouchy waterfront, a lovely area by the lake with parks, gardens, and cafes.

Take an early train from Geneva to Lausanne, visit the Olympic Museum, explore Lausanne Cathedral, have lunch by the lake, stroll along the Ouchy waterfront, and return to Geneva by train in the evening.

Chamonix, France:

Chamonix is a famous ski resort town at the base of Mont Blanc, about an hour and a half away by car or bus from Geneva. A round trip by bus costs about **50 EUR**. Start your day by taking the **Aiguille du Midi cable car** for breathtaking views of Mont Blanc and the surrounding Alps. The cable car operates from 8:10 AM to 4:30 PM, with tickets costing about **65 EUR**. The ride takes you to a height of 3,842 meters, offering panoramic views. After the cable car ride, explore the charming town of Chamonix, known for its lovely shops, cafes, and alpine atmosphere. For lunch, enjoy hearty mountain cuisine at a local restaurant. In the afternoon, if you visit in winter, enjoy skiing or snowboarding on some of the best slopes in the Alps. Alternatively, take a scenic walk along trails offering beautiful views of the mountains and valleys.

Drive or take a bus from Geneva to Chamonix, start with the Aiguille du Midi cable car, explore Chamonix town, have lunch, enjoy winter sports or scenic walks, and return to Geneva by early evening.

CHAPTER 4
BERN

Bern, the capital of Switzerland, is a place where history and modern life blend perfectly. Founded in 1191 by Duke Berchtold V of Zähringen, the city has kept its medieval charm, earning it a UNESCO World Heritage site status. Walking through the old town, you feel like you've stepped back in time.

Legend says the city was named after a bear, the first animal the Duke saw during a hunt. This story lives on at the Bear Park, where you can see bears in a natural setting right next to the Old Town. Imagine watching these amazing animals and feeling connected to the city's roots. Very Beautiful!

As the political center of Switzerland, the city hosts the Swiss federal government and many international organizations. The **Bundeshaus**, or Federal Palace, is where the Swiss Federal Assembly meets. You can take a tour to see the grand halls and learn about the Swiss political system. The architecture is stunning, and the view from the dome is incredible.

One of the city's most famous landmarks is the **Zytglogge**, a medieval clock tower from the 13th century. The clock has an astronomical calendar and animated figures that move every hour. Watching the figures come to life and hearing the clock chime is a magical experience.

The city sits along the **Aare River**, offering beautiful views and scenic walking paths. Picture yourself strolling by the river, with the water on one side and the old town's beautiful buildings on the other. The sandstone buildings and arcades are wonderfully preserved, making you feel the city's rich history as you explore.

For art lovers, the **Kunstmuseum** is a must-visit. It has art from the Middle

Ages to today, including works by Paul Klee, who lived in the city. Nearby, the **Zentrum Paul Klee** is dedicated to his works. Standing before a Klee painting, you can truly appreciate his unique art style.

If you love science, the **Einstein Museum** inside the Bern Historical Museum offers a look into the life and work of Albert Einstein. He developed his theory of relativity while living here. Walking through the exhibits, you get a sense of his genius and the impact of his discoveries.

The **Federal Palace** is another important spot. Imagine touring its grand halls where important decisions are made. The architecture is impressive, and the history inside these walls is fascinating.

The city's markets, like the **Bundesplatz market** and the **Onion Market (Zibelemärit)**, are lively places where you can experience local culture. Picture yourself exploring stalls filled with fresh produce and local crafts, soaking in the vibrant atmosphere.

The city's central location makes it a great base for exploring nearby areas. The **Emmental Valley**, known for its rolling hills and Emmental cheese, offers a beautiful countryside escape. Imagine a day trip to the valley, enjoying the scenic views and tasting delicious cheese.

TOP ATTRACTIONS

Zytglogge (Clock Tower) is right in the middle of the old town at Kramgasse 49. Take tram lines 6, 7, 8, or 9 to the "Zytglogge" stop, then walk a short distance. This old clock tower has been here since the 13th century. The clock shows the time and has figures that move every hour. When you visit, you can watch the figures come to life and hear the clock chime. Climb up inside the tower to see the intricate clockwork mechanism and enjoy a great view of the old town from the top. It's a fascinating look into medieval engineering and the city's history. Wear comfortable shoes because there are lots of steps inside the tower.

Bern Cathedral (Münster) is the tallest cathedral in Switzerland. To get there, take tram lines 6, 7, 8, or 9 to the "Zytglogge" stop and follow the signs. The cathedral has beautiful stained glass windows and a large organ. When you step inside, you'll be struck by the high vaulted ceilings and the peaceful atmosphere. For a breathtaking experience, climb the tower, which is open from 10 AM to 4 PM. The tower climb is steep with over 300 steps, but the panoramic views of the city and the Alps are well worth it. **Entry to the cathedral is free**, but the tower climb costs **5 CHF** for adults and **2 CHF** for children. Visit early to avoid crowds and bring your camera for photos from the top.

Federal Palace of Switzerland (Bundeshaus) is at Bundesplatz 3. Walk there from the main train station (Bern Hauptbahnhof) or take tram lines 3, 5, 6, 7, 8, or

9 to the "Bundesplatz" stop. This building is where the Swiss Federal Assembly meets. Inside, you can see the grand chambers where important decisions are made. The architecture is impressive, with beautiful murals and detailed carvings. Stroll through the public areas to get a sense of the political life and history of the country. **Bring your ID** for security checks if you want to enter.

Bear Park (BärenPark) is located at Grosser Muristalden, along the Aare River. Take bus line 12 to the "Bärenpark" stop. The park is a large, natural space where you can see bears roaming, playing, and swimming in a setting that mimics their natural habitat. The park is open all day, but the best time to visit is during daylight hours when the bears are most active. **Entrance to the park is free**. Spend time walking around the park to see the bears from different angles. Bring binoculars for a closer look, and take your time at the various viewpoints to get great photos. The park is perfect for families.

PLACES TO EAT

Kornhauskeller

Kornhauskeller is in the old town at Kornhausplatz 18. Take tram lines 6, 7, 8, or 9 to the "Zytglogge" stop and walk a short distance. Inside, you'll see beautiful vaulted ceilings. **Try the Berner Platte**, a big plate of meats, sausages, sauerkraut, and potatoes. For dessert, have the **Nusstorte**, a walnut tart. Main courses cost around **40-60 CHF**, and desserts are **10-15 CHF**. The wine list is excellent, featuring many Swiss wines. You may want to **Reserve a table** before you go, especially on weekends.

Restaurant Rosengarten

Restaurant Rosengarten is at Alter Aargauerstalden 31. Take bus line 10 to the "Rosengarten" stop and walk a bit. This place offers great views of the city. **Order the Zürcher Geschnetzeltes**, veal in a creamy mushroom sauce with Rösti. For dessert, try the homemade **apple strudel** with vanilla sauce. Main courses are **30-50 CHF**, and desserts are **12 CHF**. The terrace is perfect for enjoying the view. **Visit at sunset** for a nice view.

Della Casa

Della Casa is at Schauplatzgasse 16, near the main train station (Bern Hauptbahnhof). You can also take tram lines 3, 5, 6, 7, 8, or 9 to the "Bundesplatz" stop. This cozy restaurant is known for Swiss dishes. **Try the Cheese Fondue**, a blend of local cheeses with bread for dipping. Another favorite is the **Schnitzel Bernoise**, a pork cutlet with creamy mushroom sauce. For dessert, get the **Meringues with Double Cream**. Main courses are **25-40 CHF**, and desserts are **10-12 CHF**.

Altes Tramdepot

Altes Tramdepot is at Grosser Muristalden 6, next to the Bear Park. Take bus line 12 to the "Bärenpark" stop. This brewery and restaurant offer fresh, house-brewed beers. **Try the Bernese sausages with Rösti**. For dessert, have the **beer ice cream**. Main courses are **20-35 CHF**, and desserts are **8-12 CHF**. The terrace offers views of the old town and the Bear Park. **Great for a casual meal or drinks with friends**.

Metzgerstübli

Metzgerstübli is at Gurtengasse 2, near the main train station (Bern Hauptbahnhof). You can also take tram lines 3, 5, 6, 7, 8, or 9 to the "Heiliggeistkirche" stop. This small restaurant serves simple Swiss dishes. **Try the Bratwurst with onion sauce and Rösti**. For dessert, get the **caramel flan**. Main courses are **20-30 CHF**, and desserts are **8-10 CHF**. The cozy atmosphere and friendly service make it great for a quiet meal. **Arrive early or make a reservation** since it's a small place.

WHERE TO STAY

Old Town (Altstadt)

If you want to be right in the heart of things, stay in the Old Town. You can walk to all the main sights like the Zytglogge clock tower, Bern Cathedral, and Bear Park.

Hotel Bellevue Palace is located at Kochergasse 3-5. You can take tram lines 6, 7, 8, or 9 to the "Zytglogge" stop and it's just a short walk from there. It's a bit pricey, around **400-600 CHF** per night, but it's open all year and offers great views of the Alps and the River Aare. The hotel has a restaurant, bar, and fitness center. Tourists really like it because of its historic charm and excellent service. You'll find plenty of shops, cafes, and the Federal Palace nearby.

Hotel Goldener Schlüssel is at Rathausgasse 72. It's also near the "Zytglogge" stop, so you can easily get there by tram lines 3, 5, 6, 7, 8, or 9. This place offers cozy rooms at a more affordable price, around **150-250 CHF** per night. It's open year-round and has a restaurant plus free Wi-Fi. It's a favorite for its central location and charming atmosphere. Nearby, you'll find lots of restaurants, the Zytglogge clock tower, and the Town Hall.

Bern Backpackers Hotel Glocke is at Rathausgasse 75. You can walk from the main train station or hop on tram lines 3, 5, 6, 7, 8, or 9 to the "Zytglogge" stop. It's a budget-friendly option with simple rooms and a communal kitchen, perfect if you're traveling on a tighter budget. Prices range from **40-100 CHF** per night. It's open year-round and offers free Wi-Fi, a common room, and laundry facilities. It's popular with solo travelers and groups looking for affordability and a central location. Nearby, you'll find plenty of cafes, shops, and the Bern Historical Museum.

Langgasse

If you prefer a quieter neighborhood that's still close to the action, Langgasse might be your best bet.

Hotel Savoy is located at Neuengasse 26. It's a short walk from the main train station. This hotel offers modern rooms and great amenities. Prices are around **250-400 CHF** per night. It's open all year and has a restaurant, bar, and fitness center. Tourists like it for its comfort and its proximity to the Botanical Garden and several nice cafes and shops.

Hotel National can be found at Hirschengraben 24. From the main train station, take tram line 9 to the "Schönburg" stop. This hotel offers comfortable rooms and a delicious breakfast. Prices range from **120-180 CHF** per night. It's open all year and has a restaurant, bar, and free Wi-Fi. It's known for its cozy atmosphere and good value. Nearby attractions include the University of Bern and the Reitschule cultural center.

Hotel La Pergola is located at Belpstrasse 43. Take bus line 10 to the "Laubegg" stop from the main train station. It's a budget-friendly option with basic rooms in a peaceful area. Prices are around **80-120 CHF** per night. It's open all year and offers free Wi-Fi and a garden. Budget travelers appreciate its affordability and quiet location. Nearby, you'll find parks and local shops.

Kirchenfeld

Kirchenfeld is known for its museums and green spaces, making it a great choice if you enjoy culture and nature.

Swissôtel Kursaal Bern is at Kornhausstrasse 3. Take tram line 9 to the "Kursaal" stop. This luxury hotel offers stylish rooms and a spa with beautiful city views. Prices are around **200-350 CHF** per night. It's open all year and has a restaurant, bar, casino, and fitness center. Tourists love it for its luxury amenities and central location near the Bear Park and Rosengarten.

Hotel Ambassador is at Seftigenstrasse 99. From the main train station, take tram line 9 to the "Schönburg" stop. This mid-range hotel offers comfortable rooms and an indoor pool. Prices range from **150-200 CHF** per night. It's open year-round and has a restaurant, bar, and free Wi-Fi. It's popular for its value and amenities, with nearby attractions including the Gurten funicular and the Tierpark Dählhölzli.

Bed & Breakfast Villa Alma is at Thunstrasse 33. Take tram line 6 to the "Thunplatz" stop. This cozy B&B offers homely rooms and a friendly atmosphere. Prices are around **70-100 CHF** per night. It's open year-round and has free Wi-Fi and a garden. It's popular with budget travelers for its affordability and welcoming environment. Nearby attractions include the Historical Museum and the Botanical Garden.

Breitenrain

Breitenrain is a lively neighborhood known for its shops, cafes, and parks.

Hotel Allegro Bern is located at Kornhausstrasse 3. Take tram line 9 to the "Kursaal" stop. This luxury hotel offers modern rooms and a casino. Prices are around **250-400 CHF** per night. It's open year-round and has a restaurant, bar, fitness center, and spa. It's a favorite for its entertainment options and facilities, with nearby attractions including the Bear Park and Rosengarten.

Sorell Hotel Arabelle is at Mittelstrasse 6. You can walk from the main train station or take tram lines 6, 7, 8, or 9 to the "Bollwerk" stop. This mid-range hotel offers comfortable rooms and a delicious breakfast. Prices range from **120-180 CHF** per night. It's open all year and has free Wi-Fi and a business center. It's popular for its comfort and value, with nearby attractions including the Botanical Garden and several cafes.

Hotel Waldhorn is at Waldhöheweg 2. From the main train station, take tram line 9 to the "Breitenrain" stop. This budget-friendly hotel offers simple rooms close to public transport. Prices range from **90-130 CHF** per night. It's open year-round and has free Wi-Fi and a breakfast room. It's a popular choice for budget travelers due to its convenience and affordability, with parks and local shops nearby.

DAY TRIPS

Gruyères

Take a train to Gruyères, which takes about an hour and a half. When you arrive, start your day at **Gruyères Castle**, located in the medieval village. The castle is open from 9 AM to 6 PM in the summer and 10 AM to 5 PM in the winter. Tickets cost **12 CHF**. Explore the castle's rooms, which display medieval art and history. After touring the castle, walk through the charming cobblestone streets of the village. For lunch, try a restaurant like **Le Chalet de Gruyères**, where you can enjoy traditional Swiss dishes like **Gruyère cheese fondue**. In the afternoon, visit the **HR Giger Museum**, dedicated to the Swiss artist who designed the "Alien" movie. The museum is open from 10 AM to 6 PM, and tickets are **12.50 CHF**. If you have extra time, take a short bus ride to the **Maison Cailler** chocolate factory in Broc. Tours include tastings and cost around **12 CHF**.

Thun

A quick 30-minute train ride will take you to Thun. Begin by exploring the **Thun Old Town** with its picturesque streets and beautiful buildings. Visit **Thun Castle**, which offers panoramic views of the town and Lake Thun. The castle is open from 10 AM to 5 PM, and tickets cost **10 CHF**. Have lunch at a lakeside restaurant like **Restaurant Dampfschiff**, where you can enjoy fresh fish from the lake. In the afternoon, consider taking a boat cruise on Lake Thun. Cruises offer various ticket options, usually ranging from **20-40 CHF** depending on the length of the trip. These cruises are a wonderful way to see the landscape and charming villages along the shore.

Murten

Catch a train to Murten, which takes about 30 minutes. Start your day in the **Murten Old Town**, known for its well-preserved medieval architecture. Walk along the town walls for fantastic views of the lake and surrounding countryside. Visit the **Murten Museum** to learn about the town's history, including the famous Battle of Murten. The museum is open from 10 AM to 5 PM, and tickets are **10 CHF**. For lunch, try **Restaurant Chesery**, known for its local specialties like **Murten fish**. Spend your afternoon by **Lake Murten**. Rent a bike from a local shop and ride around the lake or take a leisurely stroll along the shore. The area is perfect for picnics and enjoying the peaceful environment.

Emmental

Take a train to Burgdorf, which takes about 20 minutes, then a short bus ride to **Affoltern im Emmental**. Visit the **Emmental Show Dairy** to see how Emmental cheese is made. The dairy is open from 9 AM to 5 PM, and tours cost **15 CHF**. Watch cheese-making demonstrations and taste different types of cheese. After the dairy, explore the scenic **Emmental Valley**. Have lunch at a local farmhouse restaurant like **Restaurant Hirschen**, where you can try traditional Swiss dishes. Spend the afternoon hiking or biking through the beautiful countryside, with trails that offer stunning views of rolling hills and quaint farms.

Fribourg

A 20-minute train ride brings you to Fribourg. Begin your visit in the **Fribourg Old Town**, with its narrow streets and historic buildings. Visit the **Fribourg Cathedral**, which offers stunning views from its tower. The cathedral is open from 9 AM to 6 PM, and entry is free, though the tower climb costs **5 CHF**. Have lunch at a local bistro like **Café du Midi** and try the **Fribourg sausage**. In the afternoon, visit the **Espace Jean Tinguely - Niki de Saint Phalle Museum**, which features modern art by these famous artists. The museum is open from 11 AM to 6 PM, and tickets are **12 CHF**. Enjoy a walk along the **Sarine River**, where you can see picturesque bridges and old houses.

Neuchâtel

A 40-minute train ride takes you to Neuchâtel. Visit the **Neuchâtel Castle**, which houses an archaeological museum. The castle is open from 10 AM to 5 PM, and tickets are **8 CHF**. Walk through the **Neuchâtel Old Town** and enjoy the architecture, with highlights like the **Collégiale Church**. Have lunch by **Lake Neuchâtel** at a restaurant like **Brasserie Le Cardinal**, where you can try the local **Neuchâtel sausage**. In the afternoon, visit the **Laténium**, an archaeological park and museum with exhibits from prehistoric to Roman times. The museum is open from 10 AM to 5 PM, and tickets are **9 CHF**. End your day with a relaxing boat ride on the lake, which offers beautiful views of the surrounding mountains and vineyards.

CHAPTER 5
BASEL

Y ou're visiting a city where Switzerland, Germany, and France meet. This special location makes the city full of culture and history. The Rhine River flows through, giving you beautiful views and a lively port.

The city's history goes back over two thousand years to Roman times. In the Middle Ages, it became a center for learning and trade because of its spot on the Rhine. As you walk around, you'll see modern buildings next to old medieval ones.

Visit the **Basel Minster**, a big Gothic cathedral with two tall towers. It was built between the 12th and 15th centuries. You can get great views of the city and the Rhine from its terrace. Inside, you'll find beautiful stained glass windows and a peaceful atmosphere. Nearby, the **Old Town** has narrow streets and historic buildings. Check out **Spalentor**, an old city gate, and **Marktplatz**, where you'll find the Town Hall with its bright red facade.

If you love art, this city is perfect for you. The **Kunstmuseum Basel** has lots of art from the Renaissance to modern times, including works by Picasso, van Gogh, and Monet. The museum is open from 10 AM to 6 PM, and tickets cost around **20 CHF**. The **Fondation Beyeler** shows modern art in a lovely setting and is located in Riehen, just a short tram ride away. The **Tinguely Museum** has fun, moving sculptures made by Jean Tinguely and is located near the Rhine. It's open from 11 AM to 6 PM, and tickets are **18 CHF**.

Every spring, the city hosts **Art Basel**, one of the top art fairs in the world. It attracts art lovers from everywhere and makes the city very lively. In February or March, there's the **Basel Carnival (Fasnacht)**, with parades, costumes, and music, creating a vibrant atmosphere. The carnival starts with "Morgestraich," an early morning parade at 4 AM, and continues with events throughout the week.

Because it's close to Switzerland, Germany, and France, you can easily visit nearby places like Zurich, Strasbourg, and Freiburg. The **EuroAirport Basel-Mulhouse-Freiburg** makes travel easy with many flights to other European cities.

For some nature, visit the **Botanical Garden**, one of the oldest in the world, right in the city center. The garden is open daily from 8 AM to 6 PM, and entry is free. The **Rheinpromenade** along the river is great for a walk or bike ride, with lovely views and places to relax. You can also take a ferry across the Rhine, which is a fun way to see the city from the water.

If you're into shopping, head to **Freie Strasse**, the main shopping street, where you'll find a mix of high-end boutiques and popular retail stores. For local goods and a more traditional shopping experience, visit the **Markthalle**, a large market hall with a variety of food stalls and local products.

When it comes to food, the city offers a wide range of options. Try **Rösti**, a Swiss potato dish, at a local restaurant. For a sweet treat, have some **Basler Läckerli**, a traditional gingerbread cookie.

TOP ATTRACTIONS

Basel Minster

Find Basel Minster at Münsterplatz 1. Take tram lines 2, 8, 10, or 11 to the "Bankverein" stop and walk through the old town. This Gothic cathedral, built between the 12th and 15th centuries, has two tall towers. Climb them for great views of the city and the Rhine River. Inside, you'll see beautiful stained glass windows and amazing architecture. The cathedral is open from 10 AM to 5 PM daily. It's free to enter, but climbing the towers costs **5 CHF**. Don't miss the Pfalz terrace behind the cathedral for a peaceful spot with stunning views. Nearby, you can also explore the pretty Münsterplatz square and its surrounding historic buildings.

Art Museum Basel (Kunstmuseum Basel)

Go to St. Alban-Graben 16 to visit the Art Museum Basel. Take tram lines 2 or 15 to the "Kunstmuseum" stop. The museum has three buildings: Hauptbau, Neubau, and Gegenwart. Start in the Hauptbau to see art by Picasso, van Gogh, and Monet. Then, go to Neubau and Gegenwart for modern art. The museum is open from 10 AM to 6 PM Tuesday to Sunday, and until 8 PM on Wednesday. It's closed on Mondays. Tickets are **26 CHF** for adults and free for children under 12. Plan to spend a few hours here and check for special exhibitions during your visit. There is also a lovely café in the museum where you can take a break and enjoy a snack or drink.

Tinguely Museum

Visit the Tinguely Museum at Paul Sacher-Anlage 2. Take tram lines 1, 2, or 15 to the "Riehenring" stop and walk a bit. This museum is all about the kinetic art of Jean Tinguely. You'll see moving sculptures and fun, interactive installations. The museum is open from 11 AM to 6 PM Tuesday to Sunday and is closed on Mondays. Tickets are **18 CHF** for adults, **12 CHF** for students, and free for children under 16. Don't miss the outdoor sculpture park along the Rhine. Check out the museum shop for unique souvenirs. There is also a nice riverside café where you can relax and enjoy the views after your visit.

Zoo Basel

Zoo Basel, also called Zolli, is at Binningerstrasse 40. Take tram lines 10 or 17 to the "Zoo Dorenbach" stop. The zoo is one of the oldest in Switzerland and has lots of animals like lions, elephants, and gorillas. Visit the lion enclosure, aquarium, and monkey house. The zoo is open daily from 8 AM to 6:30 PM in summer and from 8 AM to 5:30 PM in winter. Tickets are **21 CHF** for adults and **10 CHF** for children. Spend at least half a day here and enjoy a meal at one of the zoo's cafes. The zoo also has a petting area for kids and beautiful garden areas to explore.

BEST PLACES TO EAT

Restaurant Kunsthalle

When you're hungry and want a great meal, head to Restaurant Kunsthalle at Steinenberg 7. Take tram lines 6, 10, or 17 to the "Theater" stop and walk a short distance. This restaurant mixes traditional Swiss and modern food. Try Zürcher Geschnetzeltes, which is tender veal in a creamy mushroom sauce with crispy Rösti. For dessert, try the Apfelstrudel, a warm apple pastry served with vanilla ice cream. The outdoor terrace is lovely on warm evenings. Main courses cost around 30-50 CHF. They offer excellent service, and it's a good idea to make a reservation because it's popular. The ambiance is elegant, making it perfect for a relaxed evening.

Les Trois Rois

For a fancy dining experience, go to Les Trois Rois at Blumenrain 8. Take tram lines 6 or 8 to the "Schifflände" stop. The Cheval Blanc restaurant here has three Michelin stars and serves exquisite French cuisine. Try the Foie Gras or Lobster, paired with fine wines. For dessert, the Crème Brûlée is a must-try. Main courses are 50-100 CHF. You need to make a reservation as it's very popular. The restaurant offers top-notch service and stunning views of the Rhine River, adding to the luxurious dining experience.

Restaurant Schlüsselzunft

For a meal in a historic place, visit Restaurant Schlüsselzunft at Freie Strasse 25. Take tram lines 6, 8, or 11 to the "Marktplatz" stop and walk a bit. This restaurant offers Swiss and Mediterranean dishes in a building from the 13th century. Try Basler Mehlsuppe, a hearty flour soup, or Zanderfilet, a pike-perch fillet. For dessert, indulge in Meringues with double cream from Gruyères. Main courses cost around 30-60 CHF. The cozy and elegant setting is perfect for a special dinner. They have a good wine selection and the service is friendly and professional.

Volkshaus Basel

If you want a trendy and relaxed spot, go to Volkshaus Basel at Rebgasse 12-14. Take tram lines 8 or 14 to the "Volkshaus" stop. The menu has modern European food with local ingredients. Enjoy Ravioli with Ricotta and Spinach or Beef Tartare in a stylish setting. For dessert, the Chocolate Fondant is delicious. Main courses are about 25-45 CHF. The vibrant atmosphere and chic interior make it a favorite. They offer great service and have a nice selection of cocktails.

Restaurant Safran Zunft

For traditional Swiss food in a historic setting, visit Restaurant Safran Zunft at Gerbergasse 11. Take tram lines 6, 8, or 11 to the "Marktplatz" stop. Try rich, cheesy Fondue and crispy Rösti. For dessert, you can't miss the Basler Läckerli ice cream. Main courses are around 30-50 CHF. The elegant and historic charm makes it great for a hearty Swiss meal. The service is attentive, and they offer a good selection of Swiss wines.

Markthalle Basel

For a casual dining experience, go to Markthalle Basel at Viaduktstrasse 10. Take tram lines 1 or 2 to the "Markthalle" stop. This market hall has many food stalls with international and local dishes. Try local favorites like Basler Läckerli, a gingerbread cookie, and Raclette, a melted cheese dish. You can also enjoy other dishes like Indian curry or Italian pasta. Prices are about 10-20 CHF. The lively market atmosphere is perfect for trying different foods. There is communal seating, making it a social dining experience.

Klara

Another fun food hall is Klara at Clarastrasse 13. Take tram lines 6, 8, or 14 to the "Claraplatz" stop. You can try dishes from around the world like Thai Curry or Italian Pizza. For dessert, have a Gelato from the Italian stall. Main courses cost 15-30 CHF. The communal seating and diverse food options make it a social and lively dining experience. They also offer various drinks, including craft beers and exotic cocktails.

WHERE TO STAY

Old Town (Altstadt)

If you want to be close to the main attractions like Basel Minster, Marktplatz, and the Rhine River, staying in the Old Town is perfect. This area has charming cobblestone streets and historic buildings.

At Grand Hotel Les Trois Rois on Blumenrain 8, you can enjoy luxury with stunning views of the Rhine River. This historic hotel, reachable by taking tram lines 6 or 8 to the "Schifflände" stop, offers rooms from 500-1500 CHF per night. It's perfect if you want top-notch service and elegant decor. Dining at the Cheval Blanc restaurant is a treat, with dishes like Foie Gras and Lobster.

For a mid-range option, Hotel Basel at Münzgasse 12 offers comfort and convenience. Take tram lines 6, 8, or 11 to the "Marktplatz" stop and walk a short distance. Rooms here cost between 150-300 CHF per night. The hotel is known for its friendly staff and clean rooms. You'll be close to many attractions, making it easy to explore on foot.

For a budget-friendly choice, Hotel Rochat at Petersgraben 23 is near the University of Basel. You can take tram lines 3 or 8 to the "Universität" stop. Rooms range from 100-200 CHF per night. Guests love the value for money and the helpful staff. The hotel offers simple, clean rooms and a quiet garden, making it a great option if you want to save money without compromising on location.

Clara and Wettstein Quarters

These neighborhoods are just across the river from the Old Town and provide a quieter setting while still being close to major attractions.

Hotel Krafft Basel, located at Rheingasse 12, combines modern comfort with historic charm. Take tram lines 6, 8, or 14 to the "Rheingasse" stop. Rooms with beautiful river views cost between 200-400 CHF per night. The service here is excellent, and you can enjoy meals at the hotel's restaurant, which serves local and seasonal dishes.

For a mid-range stay, Hotel Balade at Klingental 8 is a good option. It's in the vibrant Clara quarter, accessible by tram lines 6, 8, or 14 to the "Rheingasse" stop. Rooms cost between 120-250 CHF per night. The hotel offers modern amenities and is known for its friendly service and clean rooms. It's a short walk from many attractions, and there's a bar where you can relax after a day of sightseeing.

If you're on a budget, Hotel Wettstein at Grenzacherstrasse 8 in the quiet Wettstein quarter is perfect. Take tram line 2 to the "Wettsteinplatz" stop. Rooms cost between 100-200 CHF per night. The hotel is appreciated for its friendly staff and peaceful location. Guests enjoy free bike rentals and a nice garden. It's a great base for exploring both the city center and Messe Basel.

Gundeldingen

Gundeldingen, a residential area south of the city center, offers green spaces and a local vibe. It's ideal if you want a quieter stay but still want to be close to the action.

GAIA Hotel, located at Centralbahnstrasse 13 next to the main train station (SBB), focuses on sustainability and comfort. Rooms cost between 150-300 CHF per night. Guests love the eco-friendly approach, excellent breakfast, and convenient location. The hotel is easily reachable from anywhere in the city. It's a highly rated choice with a wellness area that includes a sauna and fitness center.

For a budget option, Hotel City Inn at Centralbahnplatz 14 is also near the main train station. Rooms are simple and modern, priced between 90-180 CHF per night. This hotel is great for travelers needing easy access to public transport. Guests appreciate the location, value for money, and friendly staff.

Another peaceful choice is Hotel Bildungszentrum 21 at Missionsstrasse 21, set in a large park. Take tram line 15 to the "Bernerring" stop. Rooms cost between 120-220 CHF per night. Guests enjoy the spacious grounds, friendly staff, and tranquil setting. The hotel provides a relaxing escape from the city's hustle and bustle, with an on-site restaurant offering dishes made from fresh, local ingredients.

DAY TRIPS

Colmar, France is a charming town in the Alsace region. Take a direct train from Basel SBB to Colmar, which takes about 45 minutes. Trains run every hour starting from around 6:00 AM. When you get there, explore the old town with its colorful buildings. Visit the Unterlinden Museum to see the Isenheim Altarpiece, with tickets costing around €13. The museum is open from 9:00 AM to 6:00 PM. Take a boat ride through Little Venice, a lovely area with canals and flowers. Boat rides are available from 10:00 AM to 5:00 PM. For lunch, try Alsatian dishes like tarte flambée or choucroute garnie, costing €15-€30. In the afternoon, shop for souvenirs and try a slice of kugelhopf, a traditional cake.

Lucerne, Switzerland is a beautiful city with a lake and mountains. Take a direct train from Basel SBB to Lucerne, which takes about one hour. Trains run every 30 minutes starting from around 5:00 AM. Walk across the Chapel Bridge, a wooden bridge with paintings showing the city's history. Visit the Lion Monument, which is free and open all day. Take a boat cruise on Lake Lucerne for stunning views, with tickets costing CHF 25-35. Boat cruises run from 9:00 AM to 6:00 PM. For lunch, try fondue or raclette at a lakeside restaurant, costing CHF 20-40. In the afternoon, visit the Swiss Transport Museum, with tickets costing CHF 32 for adults. The museum is open from 10:00 AM to 6:00 PM.

The Black Forest, Germany is known for its woods, villages, and cuckoo clocks. Take a train from Basel SBB to Freiburg, which takes about one hour. Trains run every hour starting from around 6:00 AM. Explore the old town with cobblestone streets and colorful buildings. Visit the Freiburg Minster, a Gothic cathedral with free admission. The Minster is open from 10:00 AM to 5:00 PM. Enjoy coffee and Black Forest cake in a café, costing €5-€10. From Freiburg, take a bus or rent a car to the village of Triberg. Visit the Triberg Waterfalls, costing about €5. The waterfalls are open from 9:00 AM to 6:00 PM. Hike in the trails around Triberg or visit the Black Forest Museum, with tickets costing around €5. The museum is open from 10:00 AM to 5:00 PM.

Zurich, Switzerland, Switzerland's largest city, is a vibrant metropolis with a mix of old and new. Take a direct train from Basel SBB to Zurich, which takes about one hour. Trains run every 30 minutes starting from around 5:00 AM. Visit Bahnhofstrasse, a famous shopping street. Shops typically open from 9:00 AM to 6:00 PM. See the Grossmünster and Fraumünster churches, with free entry but a small fee to climb the towers. Both churches are open from 10:00 AM to 5:00 PM. For lunch, try Zürcher Geschnetzeltes with Rösti, costing CHF 20-40. In the afternoon, visit the Kunsthaus Zurich, with tickets costing CHF 23 for adults. The Kunsthaus is open from 10:00 AM to 6:00 PM. End your day with a walk along Lake Zurich or rent a paddle boat, costing around CHF 20 per hour. Boats are available from 9:00 AM to 7:00 PM.

Rheinfelden, Switzerland/Germany is a town on the border. Take a short train ride from Basel SBB to Rheinfelden, which takes about 20 minutes. Trains run every 30 minutes starting from around 6:00 AM. Visit the old town on the Swiss side. Cross the bridge to the German side and visit the Feldschlösschen Brewery. Brewery tours cost around CHF 20-30 and are available from 10:00 AM to 4:00 PM. In the afternoon, relax at the Rheinfelder Natursolebad, a thermal spa with pools and saunas, costing CHF 25-35. The spa is open from 9:00 AM to 9:00 PM.

Montreux, Switzerland is a town on Lake Geneva. Take a train from Basel SBB to Montreux, which takes about two hours. Trains run every hour starting from around 6:00 AM. Walk along the lakeside promenade. Visit Chillon Castle, with tickets costing CHF 13.50 for adults. The castle is open from 9:00 AM to 7:00 PM. For lunch, try perch fillets or cheese fondue, costing CHF 20-40. In the afternoon, visit the Montreux Jazz Festival site if it's festival season or take a boat cruise on Lake Geneva, costing CHF 25-35. Cruises run from 10:00 AM to 6:00 PM. Don't forget to see the Freddie Mercury statue by the lake.

Baden-Baden, Germany is a spa town. Take a train from Basel SBB to Baden-Baden, which takes about one hour and 45 minutes. Trains run every hour starting from around 6:00 AM. Visit the Caracalla Spa to relax in thermal baths and saunas, costing €15-€25. The spa is open from 8:00 AM to 10:00 PM. Walk through Lichtentaler Allee, a park with gardens. For lunch, try schnitzel with potato salad or a sausage platter, costing €15-€30. In the afternoon, visit the Baden-Baden Casino, with guided tours costing around €7.50. The casino is open from 2:00 PM to 2:00 AM. You can also take a tour of the historic Kurhaus, which hosts concerts and events.

CHAPTER 6
LUCERNE

Lucerne is a beautiful city with mountains and a big lake. It started as a small village in the 8th century and grew quickly because of the Gotthard Pass, which made it an important trade route between northern and southern Europe.

Start with the **Chapel Bridge** (Kapellbrücke). This wooden bridge, built in the 14th century, has paintings showing important moments from Lucerne's history. Walking across it is like stepping back in time. The **Water Tower**, part of the bridge, was once a prison, torture chamber, and treasury.

Next, visit the **Lion Monument** (Löwendenkmal). This sad sculpture carved into a rock honors the Swiss Guards who died during the French Revolution. Mark Twain called it "the most mournful and moving piece of stone in the world." You can really feel the sorrow when you see it.

In the **Old Town** (Altstadt), walk through medieval streets with colorful buildings and cobblestone paths. Visit **St. Peter's Chapel**, a church from the 12th century, and the **Old Town Hall** (Altes Rathaus), built in the 17th century. These places show you the city's rich history.

Lake Lucerne is very beautiful. Take a boat cruise to see stunning views of the surrounding mountains, like **Mount Pilatus** and **Mount Rigi**. You can reach these mountains by cable cars and cogwheel trains, offering amazing views and activities like hiking and skiing.

The city hosts the **Lucerne Festival**, a big event for music lovers. This famous classical music festival brings musicians and fans from all over the world. The **Fasnacht** carnival is also exciting, with colorful parades, costumes, and music filling the streets.

Visit the **Swiss Transport Museum** (Verkehrshaus der Schweiz) to see the history of transportation in Switzerland. You'll find exhibits on trains, planes, cars, and even space exploration. It's fun and interesting for all ages. I will describe each in detail.

TOP ATTRACTIONS

As i told you before, the **Chapel Bridge (Kapellbrücke)** is a must-see. Built in the 14th century, this wooden bridge crosses the Reuss River in the Old Town. It's just a five-minute walk from the train station. As you walk across, look at the paintings under the roof. These show important events from the city's history. The Water Tower, part of the bridge, has been a prison, a torture chamber, and a treasury. **Walking across Chapel Bridge feels like stepping back in time.** It's free to visit and open all day and night.

Lake Lucerne is beautiful. It's right next to the city. Go to the main pier near the train station to catch a boat cruise. These cruises range from one hour to half a day and cost CHF 25 to CHF 50. The views of the mountains, like Mount Pilatus and Mount Rigi, are amazing. You can also rent paddle boats or swim in designated areas. Walking and biking paths along the lake are great for a peaceful stroll. **A boat cruise on Lake Lucerne is a must to see the natural beauty.** Cruises run from 9:00 AM to 6:00 PM, but check the schedule for exact times.

The Lion Monument (Löwendenkmal) is very moving. It's located at Denkmalstrasse 4, near the Glacier Garden. It's a 15-minute walk from the train station, or you can take bus number 1, 19, or 22 to the "Löwenplatz" stop. This sculpture, carved into rock, honors the Swiss Guards who died during the French Revolution. **The lion looks very sad and touching.** There's no fee to visit, and it's open all day and night.

The Swiss Transport Museum (Verkehrshaus der Schweiz) at Lidostrasse 5 is fascinating. Take bus number 6, 8, or 24 from the train station, which takes about 10 minutes. The museum has exhibits on trains, planes, cars, and space travel. There are interactive displays that are fun for kids and adults. The planetarium offers shows about the stars, and the large-screen cinema shows great films. Don't miss the Swiss chocolate adventure ride, where you can learn about chocolate making and taste some delicious Swiss chocolate. **The Swiss Transport Museum is fun and educational for everyone.** It's open from 10:00 AM to 6:00 PM daily. Admission is CHF 32 for adults and CHF 12 for children. Extra fees apply for the planetarium and special exhibits.

BEST PLACES TO EAT

Old Swiss House is where you need to go for a real taste of Swiss tradition. Located at Löwenplatz 4, it's easy to find and just a short ten-minute walk from the train station. The highlight here is the **Wiener Schnitzel**, prepared right at your table, served with **Rösti**, those perfect Swiss potato pancakes. The place feels like stepping back in time with its cozy, old-world charm. Main dishes cost between CHF 30-60, but it's worth every franc. **Make sure to try the Apfelstrudel for dessert.**

Wirtshaus Galliker at Schützenstrasse 1 offers a warm, family-run atmosphere. You can walk there in about 15 minutes from the train station, or take bus number 1 or 19 to the "Schützenstrasse" stop. The must-try dish here is the **Luzerner Chügelipastete**, a delicious pastry filled with veal and mushrooms. Another favorite is the **Älplermagronen**, a hearty Swiss macaroni and cheese. Main courses range from CHF 25-40. **Don't leave without trying their homemade fruit tart.**

Restaurant Balances at Weinmarkt is the perfect spot for fine dining with a view. It's along the Reuss River and a scenic ten-minute walk from the train station. The restaurant serves a mix of Swiss and international dishes. The tasting menu is a great way to sample a variety of their offerings, with prices ranging from CHF 40-80 for main courses. The setting on the terrace, especially in the evening, is breathtaking. **Definitely go for the chocolate fondant for dessert.**

Mill'Feuille on Mühlenplatz 6 is ideal for brunch or a casual meal. It's just a quick ten-minute walk from the train station. They have a stylish, modern vibe and great views of the river. For breakfast, try the **homemade granola** and their excellent coffee. Prices for dishes are CHF 10-25. **Their house-made cakes are a must-try.**

Zunfthausrestaurant Pfistern at Kornmarkt 4 is in a historic 16th-century building, adding charm to your dining experience. It's about a ten-minute walk from the train station or you can take bus number 1 or 19 to the "Schwanenplatz" stop. The **cheese fondue** here is outstanding and a true taste of Swiss tradition. Main courses are CHF 30-60. **For dessert, the Toblerone mousse is incredible.**

Stadtkeller at Sternenplatz 3 offers a fun dining experience with Swiss folk music and traditional dishes. It's about a 15-minute walk from the train station, or you can take bus number 1 or 19 to the "Sternenplatz" stop. Try the **Raclette** or **Fondue**, perfect for sharing. Main courses are CHF 25-45. **Their homemade Swiss chocolate cake is a treat.**

Burgerstube at Hotel Wilden Mann, Bahnhofstrasse 30, is cozy with a rustic decor. It's a short ten-minute walk from the train station. You must try the

Zürcher Geschnetzeltes, a creamy veal dish with Rösti. Main courses cost CHF 30-50. **The crème brûlée is a favorite dessert.**

La Cucina at Hotel Astoria, Pilatusstrasse 29, is perfect for Italian food lovers. It's a ten-minute walk from the train station. The **wood-fired pizzas** are amazing, with a crispy crust and a variety of toppings. Main courses range from CHF 20-40. **The tiramisu is not to be missed.**

Restaurant Stern at Burgerstrasse 35 is relaxed and friendly, offering Swiss and Mediterranean dishes. It's about a ten-minute walk from the train station or you can take bus number 1 or 19 to the "Stern" stop. The **Älplermagronen**, Swiss macaroni and cheese, is a must-try. Main courses range from CHF 20-40. **Try their seasonal fruit tart for dessert.**

Seebar at Seestrasse 10 is great for a casual meal by the lake. It's a ten-minute walk from the train station. They offer light bites and drinks with stunning views. Prices are CHF 10-25. **Enjoy a scoop of local Swiss ice cream on a warm day.**

WHERE TO STAY

Old Town (Altstadt) is the best place to stay if you want to be in the heart of the action. You will be close to all the main sights like the Chapel Bridge, the Lion Monument, and the Reuss River. **Hotel des Balances**, at Weinmarkt, is a great choice if you want to stay in a fancy place. It's in a beautiful old building right by the river. The rooms are very nice, with great views. You can walk there in about 10 minutes from the train station. The rooms cost between CHF 250-450 per night. They also have a really good restaurant. If you want to save money, **Hotel Schlüssel** at Franziskanerplatz 12 is a good choice. It's also in an old building and has cozy rooms starting at CHF 100 per night. Should be perfect if you want to be in the middle of everything without spending too much. I suggest!

Staying **near the Train Station (Bahnhofplatz)** is great if you want to travel easily. You can stay at the **Radisson Blu Hotel** at Inseliquai 12. It's right next to the train station, so you don't have to carry your bags far. The hotel has modern, comfortable rooms with great views of the lake. Rooms cost between CHF 200-350 per night. If you want something cheaper, **Hotel Waldstätterhof** at Zentralstrasse 4 is a good choice. It's a short walk from the train station and has big, comfortable rooms starting at CHF 150 per night. It's a good place if you want to see the city and take day trips easily.

If you love beautiful views, you should stay **by the lake (Seeburg)**. You can stay at **Hotel Seeburg** at Seeburgstrasse 53-61. It's a 15-minute bus ride from the train station on bus number 24. The hotel has luxurious rooms with amazing views of the lake. It also has a lovely garden where you can relax. Rooms cost between CHF 200-400 per night. If you are on a budget, the **Youth Hostel Lucerne** at Sedelstrasse 12 is a great option. It's also a 15-minute bus ride from the train station on bus number 18. The hostel has dormitory beds starting at CHF 35 per night. It's good if you want to enjoy the lake views.

Tribschen is a quiet neighborhood near the Richard Wagner Museum and the lake. You can stay at **Seehotel Hermitage** at Seeburgstrasse 72. It's a 15-minute bus ride from the train station on bus number 24. The hotel has luxurious rooms with beautiful lake views and a peaceful atmosphere. Rooms cost between CHF 250-500 per night. If you want something cheaper, **Hotel Bellevue** at Seeburgstrasse 79 is a good choice. It has comfortable rooms starting at CHF 120 per night. It's a quiet and relaxing place away from the city center.

Lucerne's New Town (Neustadt) is a modern area with lots of shops and restaurants. You can stay at **Ameron Hotel Flora** at Seidenhofstrasse 5. It's just a five-minute walk from the train station and has comfortable rooms costing between CHF 150-300 per night. If you are on a budget, **Hotel Alpha** at Zähringerstrasse 24 is a good option. It has simple, clean rooms starting at CHF 80 per night. It's about a ten-minute walk from the train station, making it easy to explore the city.

DAY TRIPS

Mount Pilatus is one of the best day trips you can take. Start by taking a boat from Lucerne to Alpnachstad, which takes about 90 minutes and costs around CHF 50 for a round trip. Once you get to Alpnachstad, take the cogwheel railway to the top of Mount Pilatus. The ride costs around CHF 72 for a round trip and takes about 30 minutes. At the top, 2,132 meters high, you will have amazing views of the Swiss Alps and Lake Lucerne. There are hiking trails, a rope park, and a toboggan run. You can also eat at one of the restaurants at the top. Spend at least four to six hours here. If you visit in winter, the cogwheel railway is closed, but you can take the cable car from Kriens instead, which also costs around CHF 72.

Mount Rigi is another great day trip. Take a boat from Lucerne to Vitznau, which takes about 60 minutes and costs around CHF 50 for a round trip. From Vitznau, take the cogwheel train to the top of Mount Rigi. The train ride costs CHF 72 for a round trip and takes about 30 minutes. At the top, you will have amazing views of the lakes and mountains. There are many hiking trails and in winter, you can go sledding or skiing. You can also visit the Rigi Kaltbad Mineral

Baths & Spa. Spend four to six hours here. There are several restaurants at the top where you can enjoy Swiss food with a view.

Stanserhorn offers a fun trip with its open-top cable car. Take a train from Lucerne to Stans, which takes about 20 minutes and costs around CHF 15 for a round trip. From Stans, take a funicular railway followed by an open-top cable car to the top of Stanserhorn. The ticket costs CHF 74 for a round trip. This trip is available from mid-April to mid-November. At the top, you will find gentle hiking trails and a revolving restaurant where you can have lunch. Spend three to five hours on this trip.

Engelberg and Mount Titlis. Take a train from Lucerne to Engelberg, which takes about 45 minutes and costs around CHF 20 for a round trip. In Engelberg, take a series of cable cars to the top of Mount Titlis. The ticket costs CHF 92 for a round trip. At the top, 3,238 meters high, you can explore the Titlis Cliff Walk, visit the Glacier Cave, and take the Ice Flyer chairlift to the glacier park. There are several restaurants at the top where you can enjoy a meal. Spend six to eight hours for all the activities.

Bern, the capital city of Switzerland as i told you before, makes for a great day trip. Take a direct train from Lucerne to Bern, which takes about one hour and costs around CHF 50 for a round trip. In Bern, explore the Old Town, a UNESCO World Heritage site, with its medieval buildings and cobblestone streets. Visit the Zytglogge clock tower, the Bundeshaus (Federal Palace), and the Bear Park. Don't forgot the Bern Historical Museum and the Einstein Museum. Stroll along the Aare River and enjoy the cafes and restaurants. Try to spend six to eight hours exploring Bern.

Interlaken is perfect for outdoor activities and stunning scenery. Take a train from Lucerne to Interlaken, which takes about two hours and costs around CHF 60 for a round trip. In Interlaken, you can go paragliding, skydiving, or take a boat trip on Lake Thun or Lake Brienz. Take the Harder Kulm funicular, which costs CHF 38 for a round trip, to get a great view of the mountains and lakes. If you have time, take a short train ride to Lauterbrunnen and visit Staubbach Falls.

CHAPTER 7
LAUSANNE

When you walk through the Old Town, you'll feel like you've stepped back in time. The Gothic Cathedral is over 800 years old and very impressive. You can climb to the top for **breathtaking views of the city and the lake**. The streets around the cathedral are filled with charming cafes and shops, and every corner seems to have a story to tell.

If you go down to Ouchy, the lakeside area, you'll find beautiful parks and the **Olympic Museum**, which is great if you want to learn about the history of the Olympic Games. The museum has interactive exhibits and lots of cool artifacts. The lakeside is perfect for a relaxing walk or a boat trip on Lake Geneva, where you can enjoy stunning views of the French Alps. It's a great place to unwind and take in the scenery.

Lausanne is not about history; it's also very modern and lively. The Flon district used to be a warehouse area, but now it's full of trendy shops, restaurants, and bars. It's a great place to visit if you want to see the modern side of the city. You'll find a mix of Swiss and international food here, and the atmosphere is always lively.

The city is also known for its rich cultural scene. The **Collection de l'Art Brut** is a must-visit museum that showcases outsider art. It's different from any other art museum you've been to and offers a unique perspective on creativity. There are many festivals and events, from music and dance to film and theater.

Is also a student city, home to the University of Lausanne and the EPFL. This gives the city a youthful energy, especially in the areas around the universities, where you'll find lively bars and cafes. The presence of so many students means there's always something going on, from academic events to parties.

TOP ATTRACTIONS IN LAUSANNE

The Olympic Museum is something you absolutely have to see. To get there, just hop on the metro M2 to the Ouchy-Olympique station, then take a lovely 10-minute walk along the lake. The museum is open every day except Monday, from 9 a.m. to 6 p.m. Tickets are CHF 18 for adults and CHF 10 for students, and kids under 16 get in for free.

When you step inside, you'll be amazed by the collection of Olympic torches, medals, and athlete uniforms. They even have fun interactive displays and videos. **Make sure you don't miss the Olympic Park outside**. It's beautiful, with stunning views of Lake Geneva and the Alps. You should plan to spend about two to three hours here to really enjoy everything.

Lausanne Cathedral is right in the Old Town and is absolutely stunning. You can get there by taking the metro M2 to Riponne-Maurice Béjart station, then walk for about five minutes. The cathedral is open daily from 9 a.m. to 7 p.m., and it's free to enter. If you want an incredible view, climb the tower for CHF 5.

Inside, you'll see the most beautiful stained glass windows, and the grand pipe organ is impressive too. **Climb the tower for breathtaking views** of the city, the lake, and the mountains. It's a perfect spot for photos. Spend at least an hour here to soak in the peaceful atmosphere and the amazing views.

Ouchy Promenade is perfect for a relaxing lakeside walk. To get there, take the metro M2 to Ouchy-Olympique station. The promenade is always open and free. As you stroll along, you'll enjoy **spectacular views of Lake Geneva and the Alps**. There are beautiful gardens, fountains, and sculptures along the way.

You can rent a paddleboat or take a lake cruise from the pier, which is a wonderful way to see the area from the water. There are also many cafes and restaurants where you can sit and enjoy a meal or a coffee while watching the boats. Plan to spend a couple of hours here, especially if you want to take a boat ride or have a leisurely meal by the water.

Collection de l'Art Brut is a unique museum at Avenue des Bergières 11. Take bus number 2 or 21 and get off at the Beaulieu-Jomini stop. The museum is open daily except Monday, from 11 a.m. to 6 p.m. Tickets are CHF 12 for adults and CHF 6 for students and seniors, and children under 16 get in for free.

This museum showcases art by self-taught artists. The works are incredibly creative and different from what you usually see. Plan to spend about one to two hours here to really enjoy the unique exhibits.

Parc de Mon Repos is a beautiful park near the city center, perfect for a peaceful afternoon. You can walk there or take the bus to the Mon Repos stop. The park is open every day and is free to enter. As you walk through, you'll see lovely gardens, fountains, and statues. There's also a pretty pond with ducks and swans.

It's a great place to relax, have a picnic, or read a book. Spend at least an hour here to enjoy the calm and beauty of the park. It's a wonderful spot to take a break from the busy city and enjoy some quiet time in nature.

Esplanade de Montbenon offers stunning views and a relaxing place to unwind. It's in the city center, easy to reach by foot or by taking the metro to Lausanne-Flon station and walking for about 10 minutes. The esplanade is open all day and is free to visit.

Here, you'll find gardens and a large lawn where you can relax and enjoy the view of Lake Geneva and the Alps. There are benches and a small café where you can have a drink or a snack. It's a perfect spot to relax and enjoy the scenery. About an hour here will be great.

BEST PLACES TO EAT

Café de l'Évêché is near the Lausanne Cathedral. Take the metro M2 to Riponne-Maurice Béjart station, then walk for 5 minutes. This cozy restaurant is famous for its cheese fondue, which you should definitely try. They offer different kinds of fondue, but the classic cheese fondue is a must. For dessert, try their meringues with double cream. The atmosphere is warm and welcoming, making it a great place to unwind. The service is friendly, and the prices are reasonable, with fondue costing around CHF 25 per person. Open from 11:30 a.m. to 2 p.m. for lunch and 6:30 p.m. to 11 p.m. for dinner.

Le Chalet Suisse is on Chemin de Bonne Espérance 14. Take bus number 8 to the Val-Vert stop and walk a bit. The restaurant looks like a traditional Swiss chalet, providing a truly authentic experience. Try the raclette, which is melted cheese served over potatoes with pickles and onions. They also serve delicious fondue and other Swiss specialties. For dessert, the apple tart is a good choice. The views from the restaurant are beautiful, especially in the evening. Meals cost around CHF 30-40. Open every day from 11 a.m. to 10 p.m. The service is excellent, and the staff is very attentive.

Restaurant de l'Hotel de Ville is in the Old Town. Take the metro M2 to Bessières station, then walk for 5 minutes. This Michelin-starred restaurant serves a mix of traditional and modern dishes made with fresh, local ingredients. Try their seafood dishes or the seasonal tasting menu if you want to sample a variety of flavors. For dessert, the chocolate fondant is highly recommended. The restaurant offers fine dining with elegant service and a sophisticated atmosphere. Meals cost around CHF 100 per person. Open for lunch from 12 p.m. to 2 p.m. and for dinner from 7 p.m. to 9:30 p.m. Closed on Sundays and Mondays.

Brasserie de Montbenon is in the Esplanade de Montbenon. Take the metro to Lausanne-Flon station and walk for 10 minutes. The restaurant has a beautiful terrace with views over the lake and mountains, making it a perfect spot for a meal. Try the steak frites or the lake fish, both popular choices. For dessert, the crème brûlée is a must. The brasserie offers a mix of Swiss and French dishes with excellent service. Prices are mid-range, with meals costing around CHF 25-35. Open every day from 11:30 a.m. to 11 p.m. The ambiance is relaxed and friendly, making it a great place to dine.

Pinte Besson is at Rue de l'Ale 4, near the Lausanne Cathedral. Take the metro M2 to Riponne-Maurice Béjart station and walk for 5 minutes. This pub, dating back to 1780, is the oldest in the city and has a cozy, rustic atmosphere. Try the rosti, a Swiss potato dish, or the fondue, which is always a favorite. For dessert, the chocolate mousse is delightful. The service is warm and inviting, making you feel right at home. Meals cost around CHF 20-30. Open Monday to Saturday, 11:30 a.m. to 2 p.m. for lunch and 6 p.m. to 11 p.m. for dinner. Closed on Sundays.

Eat Me Restaurant & Cocktail Lounge is at Rue Pépinet 3, near the city center. Take the metro M2 to Lausanne-Flon station and walk for 5 minutes. This place offers small plates inspired by world cuisines, allowing you to try a variety of dishes in one meal. The lamb sliders and tuna tataki are particularly good. The cocktail menu is fantastic, with creative drinks that pair well with the food. For dessert, try the passion fruit cheesecake. The ambiance is trendy and vibrant, perfect for a night out. Small plates cost around CHF 15 each. Open Tuesday to Saturday, 6:30 p.m. to 12 a.m. Closed on Sundays and Mondays.

WHERE TO STAY

City Center

Hotel du Marché is close to Riponne-Maurice Béjart metro station, making it easy to get around. The rooms are simple and clean, with free Wi-Fi. Breakfast is available for an extra charge. Prices start at CHF 70 per night. This hotel is a good budget option and is liked by tourists for its central location. It's convenient for exploring the city's main attractions, shops, and restaurants.

Agora Swiss Night by Fassbind is near the train station. It offers modern rooms with unique decor and great views of the city and lake. The hotel has a fitness center, sauna, and free Wi-Fi. One of the highlights is the rooftop terrace where you can enjoy your morning coffee with stunning views. Prices start at

CHF 160 per night. This hotel is very convenient for public transport and popular with tourists for its comfort and amenities.

Ouchy

Beau-Rivage Palace offers stunning lake views and elegant rooms. Located in Ouchy, the hotel features beautiful gardens, a spa, several restaurants, and an outdoor pool. Prices start at CHF 500 per night. This hotel is perfect for those looking for luxury. Tourists love the beautiful views, excellent service, and luxurious atmosphere. The hotel is also close to the Ouchy Promenade, perfect for relaxing walks by the lake.

Royal Savoy Hotel & Spa is situated between the city center and Ouchy. The hotel offers a rooftop bar with amazing views, a large spa, and beautifully designed rooms. Prices start at CHF 350 per night. The mix of historic charm and modern comfort makes this hotel highly rated by visitors. It's conveniently located for exploring both the city center and the lakeside area.

Flon

Hotel des Voyageurs offers comfortable rooms with a mix of modern and classic decor. It's close to Lausanne-Flon metro station, making it very convenient for getting around. The hotel provides a good breakfast and free Wi-Fi. Prices start at CHF 150 per night. This hotel is great for those who enjoy nightlife and modern amenities. Tourists appreciate its location, comfort, and friendly service. Flon is known for its vibrant atmosphere with many shops, bars, and clubs.

Chailly

SwissTech Hotel is located in Ecublens and offers affordable, modern rooms. It's easy to reach by taking the metro M1 to the EPFL stop. The hotel is clean and comfortable, with friendly staff and all the basic amenities you need. Prices start at CHF 90 per night. Tourists like this hotel for its quiet location and convenience. It's a peaceful residential area with good public transport links to the city center.

DAY TRIPS

Montreux

Take the train to Montreux, which takes about 20 minutes. When you get there, go to **Château de Chillon**, located at Avenue de Chillon 21, 1820 Veytaux. To reach the castle, take a bus from Montreux or enjoy a 45-minute walk along the lake. The castle is open daily from 9 a.m. to 7 p.m. (April to October) and 10 a.m. to 6 p.m. (November to March). Admission is CHF 13.50 for adults and CHF 7 for children. Explore the castle's dungeons, grand halls, and towers. After the castle, stroll along the **Montreux Promenade** and visit the **Freddie Mercury statue**. Have lunch at a lakeside café with a view of Lake Geneva.

Gruyères

Catch a train to Gruyères, which takes about 1.5 hours. Start at the **Gruyères Castle**, located at Rue du Château 8, 1663 Gruyères. Walk from the train station to the castle, which takes about 15 minutes. The castle is open daily from 9 a.m. to 6 p.m. (April to October) and 10 a.m. to 5 p.m. (November to March). Admission is CHF 12 for adults and CHF 4 for children. Explore the castle's rooms and gardens. Next, visit the **HR Giger Museum**, located at Château St. Germain, Rue du Château 2, 1663 Gruyères. The museum is open daily from 10 a.m. to 6 p.m. (April to October) and 1 p.m. to 5 p.m. (November to March). Admission is CHF 12 for adults and CHF 4 for children. Have lunch at a local restaurant and try Gruyères cheese. In the afternoon, visit the **La Maison du Gruyère** cheese factory at Place de la Gare 3, 1663 Pringy-Gruyères. It's open daily from 9 a.m. to 6 p.m. Admission is CHF 7 for adults and CHF 3 for children.

Lavaux Vineyards

Take a short train ride to **Cully** or **Lutry**, about 10 minutes away. Spend the day walking or biking through the **Lavaux Vineyards**, a UNESCO World Heritage site. Enjoy the stunning views of Lake Geneva and the Alps. Visit a local winery for a wine tasting. Popular wineries include **Domaine Croix Duplex** in Grandvaux and **Domaine Bovy** in Chexbres. Have lunch at a vineyard restaurant, such as **Auberge de la Gare** in Grandvaux, which offers a beautiful view of the lake and mountains. Most wineries are open from 10 a.m. to 6 p.m., but it's best to check specific opening hours in advance.

Vevey

Take a 15-minute train ride to Vevey. Start at the **Alimentarium Food Museum** on Quai Perdonnet 25. The museum is open Tuesday to Sunday from 10 a.m. to 6 p.m. Admission is CHF 13 for adults and CHF 4 for children. Walk along the **Vevey lakeside promenade** and enjoy the views. Visit **Chaplin's World**, located at Route de Fenil 2, 1804 Corsier-sur-Vevey. Take bus number 212 from Vevey to Chaplin's World. The museum is open daily from 10 a.m. to 6 p.m. Admission is CHF 27 for adults and CHF 18 for children. Have lunch at a lakeside restaurant in Vevey, such as **Le Dézaley**, which offers local dishes and a beautiful view of Lake Geneva.

Rochers-de-Naye

Take the train to Montreux and switch to the **cogwheel train to Rochers-de-Naye**. The journey takes about 1.5 hours. The cogwheel train departs from Montreux station. At the top, you'll enjoy panoramic views of the Alps and Lake Geneva. Explore the **alpine garden** and visit the marmot enclosure. The alpine garden is open from June to September, and the marmot enclosure is open from May to October. In winter, enjoy skiing or snowshoeing. Have lunch at the mountaintop restaurant, which offers Swiss cuisine and incredible views. The restaurant is open daily from 11 a.m. to 4 p.m.

Geneva

Take the train for a 35-minute ride to Geneva. Start with a visit to the **United Nations Office**, located at Palais des Nations, 14 Avenue de la Paix. Guided tours are available Monday to Friday from 10 a.m. to 12 p.m. and 2 p.m. to 4 p.m. Admission is CHF 15 for adults and CHF 10 for children. Walk along the **Geneva Lake Promenade** to see the **Jet d'Eau** fountain, which operates daily from 10 a.m. to 11 p.m. Visit the **International Red Cross and Red Crescent Museum**, located at Avenue de la Paix 17. The museum is open daily from 10 a.m. to 5 p.m. Admission is CHF 15 for adults and CHF 7 for children. Explore the **Old Town** with its narrow streets and historic buildings. Have lunch at a café in the Old Town, such as **Café du Bourg-de-Four**, which offers Swiss and international dishes.

Yvoire

Travel by train to Nyon and then take a boat across Lake Geneva to the medieval village of Yvoire in France. The journey takes about 1.5 hours. In Yvoire, walk through the cobblestone streets and historic buildings. Visit the **Garden of Five Senses**, located at Place de la Mairie, 74140 Yvoire. The garden is open daily from 10 a.m. to 6:30 p.m. (April to October). Admission is EUR 12 for adults and EUR 7 for children. Have lunch at a restaurant with a terrace overlooking the lake, such as **Le Pré de la Cure**. Enjoy regional French cuisine and the beautiful views. Spend the afternoon exploring the village or relaxing by the water before heading back.

CHAPTER 8
INTERLAKEN

This City started as a monastery in the 12th century and became popular with tourists in the 19th century. You are on Höheweg, the main street with great views of the mountains, nice hotels, cozy cafes, and nice shops.

Think about taking a scenic train ride to Jungfraujoch, called the "Top of Europe," which is the highest train station in Europe. The trip itself is amazing, with beauriful views of the Alps. At Jungfraujoch, you can see snow and ice, even in summer. You can walk on the ice and visit the Ice Palace.

For the outdoor activities, there is a lot to do. You can hike on well-marked trails with beautiful nature all around. In winter, you can ski down snowy slopes with the mountains all around you. If you like adventure, you can try paragliding over the town and see the lakes, mountains, and town from high above.

You can also take a boat trip on Lake Thun or Lake Brienz. Visit pretty villages by the lake and explore old castles. The lakes are perfect for swimming, kayaking, or just relaxing by the water, with the mountains reflecting in the clear water.

Local parks like Höhematte are great for a picnic or a relaxing afternoon. You can sit on the grass, enjoy the mountain views, and feel the calm atmosphere. There are many places to stay, luxury hotels, guesthouses, all offering a friendly environment.

ATTRACTIONS

Jungfrau Region

Take the train from Interlaken Ost to Kleine Scheidegg, then switch to the Jungfrau Railway to Jungfraujoch, the "Top of Europe." The trip takes about 2.5 hours and costs around CHF 200. When you arrive, you will be at the highest railway station in Europe. The station is open all year from 8 a.m. to 4 p.m. Explore the Ice Palace with ice sculptures and tunnels made of ice. Visit the Sphinx Observatory for amazing views of the Aletsch Glacier, the longest glacier in the Alps. You may want to dress warmly because it is very cold at the top, even in summer. You can also try skiing or snowboarding on the snowfields. The train trip itself offers beautiful views of the Eiger, Mönch, and Jungfrau peaks, so you can do some photos. The visit through tunnels carved into the mountain is an adventure in itself for sure.

Harder Kulm

To reach Harder Kulm, go to the Harderbahn station near Interlaken Ost and take the funicular up the mountain. The ride takes about 10 minutes and costs around CHF 38 for a round-trip ticket. The funicular runs from April to November, from 9 a.m. to 9 p.m. At the top, there is a viewing platform with great views of Interlaken, the lakes, and the mountains. The platform has a glass floor section for a thrilling look down. There is also a restaurant that serves Swiss food like fondue and rosti. Sunset may be a perfect time to visit this place for nice views as the sky changes colors over the mountains and lakes. The funicular is a nice experience, climbing steeply up the mountain and offering great views along the way.

Lake Thun

Take a boat from Interlaken West to explore Lake Thun. Boats run often from April to October, and a day pass costs about CHF 64. The boat ride gives you beautiful views of the lake and mountains. Visit the town of Thun to walk through the Old Town and see Thun Castle. The castle offers panoramic views and houses a museum showcasing the region's history. In Spiez, you can walk by the lake, visit Spiez Castle, and relax in the gardens. The castle in Spiez has a beautiful park and offers insights into medieval life. Oberhofen is known for its lakeside castle, where you can tour historic rooms and gardens. The castle has a museum and a lakeside turret that offers amazing views. The lake is great for swimming, kayaking, or relaxing by the shore. There are many spots along the lake for picnics.

Lake Brienz

Go to Lake Brienz, which is on the east side of Interlaken. Take a boat from

Interlaken Ost to Brienz. Boats run from April to October, and a day pass costs about CHF 64. The water is a beautiful turquoise color, and the mountains around it are stunning. In Brienz, visit the Ballenberg Open-Air Museum to see traditional Swiss buildings and crafts. The museum is open from April to October, 10 a.m. to 5 p.m., and tickets cost CHF 28 for adults. The museum is a large open-air area with houses and buildings from different regions of Switzerland, demonstrating traditional crafts and ways of life. Take the Brienz Rothorn Railway, a steam train that goes to the top of Brienzer Rothorn. The railway runs from June to October, and tickets cost around CHF 92. At the top, enjoy the views of the Alps and Lake Brienz and have a meal at the mountain restaurant.

PLACES TO EAT

Restaurant Taverne

When you're looking for a cozy place with a delightful garden terrace, head to Restaurant Taverne inside Hotel Interlaken at Höheweg 74. It's just a **10-minute walk from Interlaken Ost train station**. The menu is full of traditional Swiss dishes. You absolutely must try the **cheese fondue**, a delicious dish where you dip bread into a pot of melted cheese. They also serve **raclette**, which is melted cheese scraped over potatoes and pickles. Another favorite is **rosti**, a Swiss potato pancake. Prices for main dishes are around CHF 25-40. The restaurant is open daily from 6:30 p.m. to 10 p.m. It's wise to **make a reservation**, especially during the busy tourist season, to ensure you get a table. The garden terrace offers a lovely view of the hotel's garden, creating a relaxing dining experience.

Husi Bierhaus

If you're looking for a lively place with a wide variety of beers and hearty meals, head to Husi Bierhaus at Höheweg 135. It's about a **10-minute walk from both Interlaken West and Interlaken Ost train stations**. The atmosphere here is friendly and welcoming. You should definitely try their **schnitzel**, a breaded and fried meat dish, or their juicy **burgers**. Prices for main dishes are around CHF 20-30. Husi Bierhaus is open daily from 11:30 a.m. to midnight. No need to make a reservation; just walk in and enjoy the lively setting. The interior is warm and rustic, with plenty of seating and a fun, casual vibe.

Ox Restaurant & Grill

For high-quality steaks and grilled dishes, go to Ox Restaurant & Grill at Am Marktplatz, Postgasse 10. From **Interlaken West train station, it's a 5-minute walk**. The meat here is cooked to perfection, so try the **rib-eye steak** or **grilled lamb chops**. They also offer a variety of sides like garlic mashed potatoes and grilled vegetables. Main dishes cost around CHF 30-50. The restaurant is open from Tuesday to Saturday, from 11:30 a.m. to 2 p.m. and 6:30 p.m. to 10 p.m. It's a good idea to **make a reservation for dinner** to ensure you get a table. The dining area is modern with a cozy atmosphere, and the service is excellent.

Ladelokal

For healthy and delicious vegetarian meals, visit Ladelokal at Postgasse 19. It's about a **10-minute walk from Interlaken West train station**. You should try their **vegetable lasagna**, which is rich and hearty, or the **quinoa salad**, which is fresh and nutritious. Main dishes are priced around CHF 20-30. The restaurant is open from Monday to Friday, 11 a.m. to 2:30 p.m. and 5:30 p.m. to 9 p.m. It's a small, cozy spot perfect for a casual meal. While reservations are not necessary, they can be helpful during peak times. The interior is bright and welcoming, making it a great spot for a relaxed meal.

Goldener Anker

Goldener Anker at Marktgasse 57 offers a warm, traditional atmosphere with a menu full of Swiss favorites. It's about a **10-minute walk from Interlaken West train station**. Be sure to try the **cheese fondue**, where you dip bread into melted cheese, or the **Zürcher Geschnetzeltes**, which is sliced veal in a creamy sauce. Main dishes cost around CHF 25-40. The restaurant is open daily from 11 a.m. to 10 p.m. It's a good idea to **reserve a table for dinner** to ensure you can enjoy your meal in this charming setting. The interior is cozy and traditional, with wooden decor and friendly service.

Vineria Perbacco

For a taste of Italy, visit Vineria Perbacco at Jungfraustrasse 28. It's about a **10-minute walk from Interlaken West train station**. The menu includes delicious pasta dishes like **homemade lasagna** and classic **Margherita pizza**. They also have an excellent selection of Italian wines to pair with your meal. Main dishes cost around CHF 20-35. The restaurant is open from Tuesday to Sunday, 11:30 a.m. to 2 p.m. and 6 p.m. to 10 p.m. **Reservations are recommended for dinner**, especially on weekends. The ambiance is warm and inviting, with a touch of Italian charm.

Taste of India Restaurant

For authentic Indian cuisine, head to Taste of India at Jungfraustrasse 46. It's about a **10-minute walk from Interlaken West train station**. You should try the **butter chicken**, a creamy and mildly spiced dish, or the **lamb curry**, which is full of robust spices. Prices for main dishes are around CHF 20-30. The restaurant is open daily from 11 a.m. to 2:30 p.m. and 5 p.m. to 11 p.m. It's a popular spot, so making a reservation is a good idea to avoid waiting. The interior is vibrant and colorful, creating an authentic Indian dining experience.

La Terrasse

For a fine dining experience, visit La Terrasse in the Victoria-Jungfrau Grand Hotel at Höheweg 41. It's about a **10-minute walk from Interlaken West train station**. The menu features gourmet Swiss and international dishes. Try the **filet mignon** or the **lobster bisque**. Prices are higher, with main dishes around CHF 40-60. The restaurant is open daily from 6:30 p.m. to 10 p.m. **Reservations are essential** for this special dining experience. The dining room is elegant with views of the gardens, and the service is impeccable.

WHERE TO STAY

Hotel Interlaken

When you're looking for a place that combines traditional Swiss with modern comforts, head to Hotel Interlaken at Höheweg 74. You can reach it with a **10-minute walk from Interlaken Ost train station**. The rooms here offer stunning views of either the garden or the majestic mountains. Prices range from CHF 150 to CHF 300 per night, depending on the season and room type. Guests rave about the friendly service, comfortable rooms, and the delightful garden terrace. You'll love starting your day with a hearty meal in such a picturesque setting. The hotel provides welcoming atmosphere, making it a favorite among tourists who appreciate its central location and excellent breakfast options.

Victoria-Jungfrau Grand Hotel & Spa

For a touch of luxury, stay at the Victoria-Jungfrau Grand Hotel & Spa, located at Höheweg 41. You'll find it with a **10-minute walk from Interlaken West train station**. This grand hotel offers breathtaking views of the Jungfrau mountain range. Prices start around CHF 500 per night, but the experience is worth every penny. The hotel features a luxurious spa, an indoor pool, gourmet restaurants, and elegant rooms. Guests consistently rate it highly for its exceptional service, beautiful decor, and top-notch amenities. Imagine indulging in a spa treatment or enjoying a gourmet meal with fantastic views. Will be perfect if you want a luxurious stay with impeccable service and panoramic views of the mountains.

Backpackers Villa Sonnenhof

For budget accommodation with a great atmosphere, check out Backpackers Villa Sonnenhof at Alpenstrasse 16. It's about a **15-minute walk from Interlaken Ost train station**. Prices for a bed in a dormitory start around CHF 35 per night, while private rooms cost around CHF 120 per night. The hostel offers free breakfast, a shared kitchen, and a cozy lounge area. Tourists love it for its cleanliness, friendly staff, and great location. This is a great choice if you're looking for affordable accommodation with a friendly atmosphere and a chance to meet other travelers. You can relax in the garden or take advantage of the free Wi-Fi and laundry facilities, making it a convenient and comfortable stay.

Hotel Bellevue

Hotel Bellevue at Marktgasse 59 is another excellent mid-range option. It's a **10-minute walk from Interlaken West train station**. The hotel offers rooms with balconies overlooking the Aare River, providing a serene and picturesque view. Prices range from CHF 150 to CHF 250 per night. Guests appreciate the comfortable rooms, beautiful river views, and the convenient location. The hotel also offers free breakfast and has a lovely garden where you can relax. You'll enjoy the peaceful ambiance and the proximity to shops and restaurants, making it a perfect base for exploring the area.

Hotel Beausite

Hotel Beausite, located at Seestrasse 16, is just a **10-minute walk from Interlaken West train station**. This charming hotel offers rooms with mountain views and a lovely garden. Prices range from CHF 120 to CHF 200 per night. Tourists rate it highly for its welcoming staff, comfortable rooms, and delicious breakfast. The hotel also provides free parking and is known for its cozy atmosphere. It's a great option if you want a comfortable stay with a homely feel, making you feel right at home while you enjoy the beautiful surroundings. The hotel's traditional decor and friendly service add to its charm, creating a relaxing and enjoyable stay.

Hotel Royal St. Georges Interlaken - MGallery

For an upscale stay, consider Hotel Royal St. Georges Interlaken at Höheweg 139. It's a **5-minute walk from Interlaken Ost train station**. Prices start around CHF 200 per night. The hotel features elegant rooms, a spa, and a fine dining restaurant. Guests love the historic charm, excellent service, and spacious rooms. It's highly recommended for its luxurious ambiance and great location close to the main attractions. You'll feel like you've stepped back in time while enjoying all the modern amenities. The hotel's grand architecture and beautiful interiors make it a unique and memorable place to stay.

Youth Hostel Interlaken

For a modern budget option, stay at Youth Hostel Interlaken at Am Bahnhof Ost, right next to **Interlaken Ost train station**. Prices for a bed in a dormitory start around CHF 40 per night, while private rooms cost around CHF 120 per night. The hostel offers a contemporary design, free breakfast, and a shared kitchen. Tourists appreciate the clean facilities, convenient location, and friendly atmosphere. It's a great budget option with easy access to public transport, making it perfect for travelers who want to explore without spending too much.

The hostel's modern amenities and social areas provide a comfortable and enjoyable stay.

Hotel Du Nord

Hotel Du Nord at Höheweg 70 is a great choice if you want a mix of comfort and convenience. It's a **5-minute walk from Interlaken Ost train station**. Prices range from CHF 150 to CHF 250 per night. The hotel offers rooms with views of the Jungfrau mountain and provides a free breakfast. Guests rate it highly for its comfortable rooms, great location, and friendly service. It's recommended for beautiful mountain views, giving you a perfect base to explore the region. The hotel's central location and comfortable amenities make it an ideal choice for your stay.

OUTDOOR ACTIVITIES

Hiking

For a great hiking experience, start with the **Harder Kulm trail**. You can get there by taking the funicular from Interlaken Ost, which runs from April to November. The round-trip ticket costs about CHF 38. Once you reach the top, the hike takes about two hours and offers amazing views of Lake Thun, Lake Brienz, and the surrounding mountains. If you want a more challenging hike, try the **Schynige Platte to First hike**. This hike takes about six hours and offers stunning alpine scenery. To reach Schynige Platte, take the cogwheel train from Wilderswil, which costs about CHF 64 for a round trip. You will need to wear sturdy boots, bring plenty of water, and i suggest you to check the weather before heading out. **The best time for hiking is from late spring to early autumn.**

Paragliding

To see the area from above, go paragliding with **Paragliding Interlaken**. You can book your flight online or at their office in town. You'll fly over lakes and mountains with a professional pilot. Flights cost around CHF 170 and last about 1.5 hours, including a 10-20 minute flight. Paragliding operates year-round, but the best conditions are from spring to autumn. Wear comfortable clothes and sturdy shoes. **This can be a perfect place to capture the beautiful views.** Of course, you hae to follow your pilot's instructions for a safe and enjoyable flight.

Water Sports

For water sports, head to Lake Thun or Lake Brienz. You can rent kayaks or stand-up paddleboards from **Hightide Kayak School**. Start your kayak experience at Bönigen on Lake Brienz, which is just a short bus ride from Interlaken Ost. Rentals cost about CHF 60 for a half-day. Paddle through the turquoise waters with a beautiful mountain backdrop. If you prefer a relaxed experience, take a boat tour on either lake. These tours operate from April to October and cost about CHF 25-35 per person. And, of course **wear a life jacket, stay close to the shore if you're inexperienced**.

Canyoning

For an adventure, join a canyoning tour with **Outdoor Interlaken**. The Grimsel Canyon is a great spot, featuring jumps, slides, and rappelling down waterfalls. Tours cost around CHF 159 and include all necessary equipment like wetsuits, helmets, and harnesses. Canyoning tours run from May to October. Meet at their office in Interlaken and they will transport you to the canyon. The best time for canyoning is from late spring to early autumn when water levels are manageable.

Biking

Visit the scenic routes around town by renting a bike from **Flying Wheels** in the town center. Rentals cost about CHF 30 per day. Ride around Lake Thun for stunning views and several places to stop for a break. The route is mostly flat and suitable for all levels. For a more challenging ride, try the trails in the nearby mountains, which offer a mix of terrain and spectacular views. Always wear a helmet, carry a map, and make sure your bike is in good condition. **Biking is best enjoyed from spring to autumn** when the weather is warm and the trails are clear.

Skiing and Snowboarding

In winter, head to the Jungfrau Region for skiing and snowboarding. Take a train from Interlaken Ost to Grindelwald or Lauterbrunnen. Ski resorts like **Kleine Scheidegg-Männlichen** and **Mürren-Schilthorn** cater to all levels, from beginner to expert. A day pass costs around CHF 75. Rentals and lessons are available at the base of the slopes. Always check the weather and avalanche conditions before heading out. Wear appropriate winter gear, including layers, gloves, and goggles. **The ski season typically runs from December to April**, providing ample time to enjoy the snow-covered peaks and pristine slopes.

Rock Climbing

Try rock climbing with **Alpin Raft** for guided tours and equipment. Popular climbing areas include the limestone cliffs near Gimmelwald and the granite walls in Grimsel Pass. Tours cost about CHF 120 and include all necessary equipment. **Summer is the best time for climbing** when the weather is stable and the rock faces are dry. Be sure that you have the right gear and know basic safety techniques.

Skydiving

For an adrenaline rush, try skydiving with **Skydive Interlaken**. Experience a tandem jump from 4,000 meters, freefalling over the Swiss Alps and lakes before the parachute opens. Skydiving is available year-round, but the best views are in the clear skies of summer and early autumn. Jumps cost around CHF 395. **The entire experience, from briefing to landing, takes about three hours**, providing a heart-pounding thrill as you plummet towards the earth before gently floating down with a panoramic view of the stunning landscape.

CHAPTER 9
ZERMATT

*Z*ermatt, nestled at the foot of the iconic Matterhorn, is a place where history and breathtaking landscapes come together. This village, which began as a modest farming community in the 19th century, gained fame when British climbers discovered its potential for alpine adventures. The turning point was in 1865 when Edward Whymper successfully conquered the Matterhorn, marking **Zermatt** as a top destination for mountaineers and adventure seekers.

Today, you can enjoy **Zermatt** all year round. One of the highlights is visiting the **Matterhorn Glacier Paradise**, accessible via the highest cable car in Europe. You can purchase a round-trip ticket for about CHF 100. This cable car runs daily from 8:30 AM to 4:30 PM. At the top, the panoramic views are simply breathtaking, and you can even ski here during summer. For who prefer a historic trip, the **Gornergrat Railway** is a must. This train ride, which has been operating since 1898, takes you through alpine landscapes to the Gornergrat summit. From here, you'll get spectacular views of the Matterhorn and surrounding peaks. A round-trip ticket costs around CHF 90, and the trains run from 7:00 AM to 8:00 PM.

As you walk through the village, you'll notice the atmosphere, thanks to **Zermatt** being car-free. This not only keeps the air clean but also maintains the peaceful charm of the village. You'll find quaint wooden chalets, luxurious hotels, and a variety of restaurants offering mouthwatering Swiss cuisine. After a day of exploring, unwind in one of the many wellness spas. If you're into hiking, the **Five Lakes Walk** is a trail you shouldn't miss. This 9-kilometer hike, taking about three hours, leads you past five beautiful lakes, each reflecting the Matterhorn's majestic presence. It's best done from June to October when the weather is ideal.

For understanding the village's history, visit the **Matterhorn Museum**. Is Located in the middle of the village, this museum provides insights into the dramatic first ascent of the Matterhorn and showcases artifacts from the past. It's open daily from 11:00 AM to 6:00 PM, with an admission fee of CHF 10.

This City also hosts fantastic events throughout the year. One standout event is the **Zermatt Unplugged music festival** in April. Imagine yourself enjoying the live music in an intimate alpine setting, surrounded by the beauty of snow-capped mountains. This festival features international artists.

ATTRACTIONS

Matterhorn

You have to see the Matterhorn up close. To do this, go to the **Matterhorn Glacier Paradise**. Take the cable car from the southern end of the village. The round-trip ticket costs about CHF 100. The cable car runs daily from 8:30 AM to 4:30 PM. At the top, you're at 3,883 meters, the highest cable car station in Europe. **The views are stunning.** Explore the ice palace with its cool ice sculptures and eat at the restaurant while you enjoy the amazing scenery. You can ski here all year round. **Dress warmly because it's very cold up there.**

Gornergrat Railway

The Gornergrat Railway is a fantastic train ride. Start at the train station in the center of the village. A round-trip ticket costs about CHF 90, and trains run from 7:00 AM to 8:00 PM. The ride to the summit at 3,089 meters takes about 33 minutes. You'll see beautiful views of the Matterhorn and other peaks along the way. When you reach the top, you can visit the observatory and have a meal at the restaurant. There are hiking trails starting from Gornergrat if you want to explore more.

Matterhorn Glacier Paradise

Matterhorn Glacier Paradise is another place you should visit. Take the cable car from the village; a round-trip ticket costs about CHF 100. The cable car operates daily from 8:30 AM to 4:30 PM. At the top, you get 360-degree views of the mountains. Visit the ice palace to see impressive ice sculptures and have a meal at the restaurant. You can ski here any time of the year.

Sunnegga Paradise

Sunnegga Paradise offers amazing views and fun activities. Take the funicular from the village center. A round-trip ticket costs about CHF 40. The funicular runs from 8:00 AM to 5:00 PM. At Sunnegga, you can see the Matterhorn, hike on scenic trails, or relax by Leisee, a small lake perfect for swimming and picnicking. There's also a restaurant where you can enjoy Swiss food with a great view.

Rothorn

To get to Rothorn, take the funicular to Sunnegga, then a gondola, and finally a cable car. The total round-trip cost is about CHF 67. The transportation runs from 8:00 AM to 4:30 PM. At 3,103 meters, Rothorn offers incredible views of the peaks and valleys. It's great for hiking in the summer and skiing in the winter. There's a restaurant at Rothorn where you can eat while enjoying the scenery. For photos, this spot is perfect.

Hörnli Hut

Hörnli Hut, also known as Hörnlihütte, is the starting point for climbers heading to the Matterhorn. Take the cable car from the village to Schwarzsee, which costs about CHF 50 for a round trip. From Schwarzsee, it's a two-hour hike to Hörnli Hut. The hut provides basic accommodations and meals, mainly for climbers. Even if you're not climbing the Matterhorn, the hike offers stunning views. The hut is open from June to September.

PLACES TO EAT

Restaurant Schäferstube

Located at the Romantik Hotel Julen, it's just a 10-minute walk from the train station. Here, you can try traditional dishes like succulent lamb specialties and classic Swiss raclette. The warm, rustic atmosphere, complete with wooden decor and a fireplace, makes it a perfect spot to relax after a day of exploring. Prices range from CHF 30 to CHF 50 per dish. To get there, walk along the main street, Bahnhofstrasse, then turn onto Riedstrasse. The hearty portions and friendly service will make you feel right at home (i am not joking). They are open daily from 11:00 AM to 10:00 PM, and it's advisable to make a reservation, especially during the busy winter season.

Chez Vrony

For an perfect dining experience with beautiful views of the Matterhorn,

Chez Vrony is a must-try. This mountain restaurant is accessible by taking the Sunnegga funicular and then enjoying a short hike. The funicular ride costs around CHF 40 round trip, and the hike takes about 20 minutes. As you dine, you can enjoy gourmet dishes like homemade sausages and an organic beef burger, with main courses priced between CHF 40 and CHF 70. The restaurant's terrace offers panoramic views that perfectly complement the exquisite food. They are open from 9:00 AM to 4:00 PM in the winter and until 5:00 PM in the summer. **Findlerhof**

Another gem nestled above Zermatt in the hamlet of Findeln is **Findlerhof**. To reach this charming restaurant, take the Sunnegga funicular and hike down a scenic path. The funicular ride costs around CHF 40 round trip, and the hike takes about 15 minutes. Known for its fantastic views and mouthwatering dishes like veal filet and crispy rosti, Findlerhof provides a cozy, traditional Swiss chalet experience. Prices range from CHF 30 to CHF 60 per dish. The combination of delicious food, a warm atmosphere, and stunning vistas makes the hike well worth it. They are open from 9:00 AM to 5:00 PM, and it's best to call ahead for reservations to ensure you get a table with a view.

Whymper-Stube

For the authentic Swiss cheese dishes, **Whymper-Stube** is the place to go. Located on Bahnhofstrasse, this restaurant specializes in fondue and raclette. The inviting, cozy interior is perfect for a relaxed dinner after a day on the slopes. Fondue prices range from CHF 25 to CHF 35 per person, offering a great value for the rich, flavorful experience. It's conveniently situated on the main street near the train station, making it very easy to find. They are open daily from 12:00 PM to 10:00 PM.

Restaurant Spycher

For a more refined dining experience, visit **Restaurant Spycher** within Hotel La Ginabelle. It's about a 15-minute walk from the train station, located on Vispastrasse. The restaurant offers a sophisticated menu featuring Swiss and international cuisine, including dishes like tender beef tenderloin and fresh seafood. Prices range from CHF 35 to CHF 70 per dish. The elegant yet welcoming atmosphere, paired with an extensive wine list, makes it an excellent choice for a special evening out. Enjoy a leisurely walk to the restaurant, which is open from 6:30 PM to 10:00 PM, and treat yourself to an unforgettable dining experience. Reservations are recommended, especially for dinner.

Snowboat

Snowboat is an excellent choice. Located near the Gornergrat Railway station, this restaurant and bar offer a diverse menu that includes sushi, burgers, and more. Prices range from CHF 20 to CHF 50 per dish, providing a range of options to suit different tastes and budgets. The outdoor terrace is perfect for enjoying a meal with views of the mountains. Snowboat's central location makes it easy to reach, and it's a great spot for both lunch and dinner. They are open daily from 11:00 AM to 10:00 PM. The lively atmosphere and creative menu make it a favorite among locals and tourists alike.

Du Pont

This is the oldest restaurant in Zermatt. Situated on Kirchplatz, near the parish church of St. Mauritius, Du Pont is famous for its hearty Swiss dishes like schnitzel and rosti. Prices are very reasonable, ranging from CHF 20 to CHF 40 per dish. The rustic decor and friendly service create a warm and inviting atmosphere, making it a wonderful place to unwind. It's easy to find and offers an authentic dining experience that reflects the rich culinary heritage of the region. They are open daily from 11:00 AM to 10:00 PM.

WHERE TO STAY

Hotel Bahnhof

For a budget stay, **Hotel Bahnhof** is a great choice. It's right next to the train station, which makes it super convenient if you have a lot of luggage. The rooms are simple, clean, and comfortable, with shared bathrooms to help keep costs down. Prices start at around CHF 50 per night. You're close to shops and restaurants, so it's easy to explore the village. The hotel is open all year, so you'll have a cozy base no matter when you visit. You'll find it very easy to get around from here, and the staff is always ready to help with any questions you have.

Hotel Alpina

If you want a quieter place, **Hotel Alpina** is a good budget option. It's about a 5-minute walk from the train station, tucked away in a peaceful part of the village. The rooms are cozy and come with free Wi-Fi, which is great for staying connected. Prices start at CHF 80 per night, and breakfast is included. This hotel is perfect for accessing both the town center and the nearby hiking trails. The peaceful surroundings ensure you'll get a good night's sleep. It's open year-round and has a lounge area where you can relax.

Hotel Alpenblick

For more comfort without breaking the bank, **Hotel Alpenblick** is a fantastic mid-range option. It's about a 10-minute walk from the train station, situated on a slight hill that gives you lovely views of the Matterhorn. The rooms are comfortable and well-appointed, ensuring you have a restful stay. The hotel features a sauna and fitness center, perfect for relaxing after a day of sightseeing or skiing. Prices start at CHF 120 per night, including breakfast. The cozy atmosphere and friendly service make this hotel a favorite among visitors. Nearby, you'll find the Gornergrat Railway and various hiking trails, making it a convenient spot for all your activities.

Hotel Bristol

For a centrally located hotel with great amenities, **Hotel Bristol** is an excellent mid-range choice. It's just a 5-minute walk from the train station and close to shops, restaurants, and ski lifts. The modern rooms have free Wi-Fi and are designed for comfort. The hotel has a wellness area with a sauna and steam bath, perfect for unwinding after an active day. Prices start at CHF 150 per night, including breakfast. This hotel is ideal for families and couples looking for comfort and convenience. It's near the main street, Bahnhofstrasse, where you'll find plenty of dining and shopping options.

Mont Cervin Palace

If you're looking to indulge in luxury, stay at **Mont Cervin Palace**. It's in the heart of the village, about a 5-minute walk from the train station. This 5-star hotel offers beautifully decorated rooms with unique charm. The hotel has a world-class spa, several fine dining restaurants, and exceptional service, ensuring a memorable stay. Prices start at CHF 500 per night, making it perfect for special occasions or a truly relaxing getaway. The central location means you're close to the action, but the hotel's amenities provide a peaceful retreat. Services include an indoor pool, fitness center, and shuttle service to the ski lifts.

The Omnia

For a luxury stay with a bit of exclusivity, choose **The Omnia**. This 5-star hotel is perched on a rock, accessible via a tunnel and elevator, offering stunning views of the mountains. The modern design and exceptional service make it a standout choice. Prices start at CHF 400 per night. The wellness center features an indoor/outdoor pool, a sauna, and a hot tub with Matterhorn views, providing a relaxing experience. It's perfect for those seeking privacy and luxury. The hotel is near the village center, making it easy to access shops, restaurants, and ski lifts while offering a secluded and serene atmosphere.

OUTDOOR ACTIVITIES

Skiing

If you love skiing, you're in for a treat. The ski season runs from late November to early May, and you can even ski on the glacier during the summer. The main ski areas are accessible via the Gornergrat Railway or the Matterhorn Glacier Paradise cable car, which both offer stunning views on your way up.

Located at Bahnhofplatz, the Gornergrat Railway station is easy to find right in the heart of Zermatt. Tickets for the railway start at CHF 63 for a round trip. The Matterhorn Glacier Paradise cable car station is located at Schluhmattstrasse, with round-trip tickets starting at CHF 95. Always wear a helmet, check the weather forecast before you go, and start early to avoid the crowds. You should buy a map of the ski runs and follow all safety signs.

Hiking

Zermatt offers some of the best hiking trails in the Alps. The best time for hiking is from June to September when the weather is warm, and the trails are clear. You can start your hike right from the village or take a funicular to Sunnegga or a cable car to Gornergrat. For Sunnegga, head to the funicular station at Vispastrasse, with tickets starting at CHF 12.50. For Gornergrat, use the same railway station as mentioned above. Popular hikes include the Five Lakes Walk, where you can see stunning reflections of the Matterhorn in the clear alpine lakes, and the trail to the Matterhorn Glacier Paradise. Wear sturdy hiking boots, bring plenty of water, and tell someone where you're going. It's also smart to carry a map or use a GPS device. Most trails are open from dawn till dusk and are free to access, though transportation to trailheads may have a cost.

Mountaineering

For experienced climbers, the Matterhorn is the ultimate challenge. The best time for mountaineering is from July to September. Proper gear, including ropes, harnesses, and ice axes, is essential. Hiring a local guide, which you can find through Alpine Center Zermatt at Bahnhofplatz, is highly recommended. Prices for a guided climb start around CHF 1500. The Hörnli Hut, the starting point for most Matterhorn climbs, is accessible via a cable car to Schwarzsee followed by a hike. The cable car station is located at Schluhmattstrasse, and tickets start at CHF 40. Always check the weather conditions before setting out and be prepared for sudden changes.

Paragliding

For beautiful aerial view of Zermatt, try paragliding. Tandem flights are available for beginners and are offered by companies such as Air Zermatt, located at Bahnhofplatz. Launch sites include Rothorn and Gornergrat. The best time for paragliding is in the summer when the weather is stable. Flights typically cost around CHF 170. Dress warmly in layers, as it can get cold up high. Book your flight with a certified instructor who provides all the necessary safety gear.

Mountain Biking

Zermatt has great trails for mountain biking, and you can rent bikes at shops like Bayard Sport at Bahnhofstrasse. The best time for biking is from June to October. Trails like the Moos Trail and the Sunnegga Trail cater to various skill levels, offering a mix of challenging descents and scenic routes. Always wear a helmet and protective gear, and ensure your bike is in good condition. Stick to marked paths and respect hikers. Bring enough water and snacks, and watch the weather, as it can change quickly in the mountains. Rental prices start around CHF 40 per day, and trails are typically open from dawn to dusk.

Rock Climbing

There are several excellent rock climbing spots around Zermatt for all skill levels. The best climbing season is from June to September. Areas like the Riffelhorn and Dossen offer fantastic climbing routes. Riffelhorn is accessible via the Gornergrat Railway, while Dossen can be reached by hiking from the village. Climbing equipment can be rented from shops like Alpin Center Zermatt. Always climb with a partner and use proper climbing gear. It's wise to check in with local climbing schools or guides for the latest information on routes and safety. Equipment rental prices start at CHF 30 per day.

Ice Skating

In winter, the natural ice rink in the village is a fun place to skate. Open from December to February, you can rent skates there for around CHF 10. The rink is located near the Zermatt School at Kirchplatz. It's great for families looking for a fun activity. The rink is open from 10 AM to 9 PM, and there's a small entry fee of CHF 5. Skating under the winter sky with the surrounding mountains as your backdrop is a magical experience.

Tobogganing

For a fun winter activity, try tobogganing on the Rotenboden to Riffelberg run. The best time for tobogganing is from December to March. You can rent a toboggan at the Rotenboden station, which you can reach by the Gornergrat Railway. It's a thrilling ride down with beautiful views of the Matterhorn along the way. The run is about 1.5 kilometers long and suitable for all ages. Toboggan rental costs around CHF 10, and the railway ticket to Rotenboden is CHF 47 one way. Afterward, you can warm up with a hot drink at one of the mountain huts.

Trail Running

Zermatt's trails are perfect for trail running, offering challenging terrain and breathtaking views. The best time for running is from May to October. Popular routes include the Zermatt Marathon route, which takes you through some of the most scenic parts of the area. Start early to avoid the midday heat and carry a small backpack with essentials like snacks and a map. Always let someone know your route and expected return time. Trails are open from dawn to dusk and are free to access.

Nordic Walking

Nordic walking is a great way to explore Zermatt's beautiful scenery at a more leisurely pace. The best time for this activity is from April to October. Many trails around Zermatt are perfect for Nordic walking, such as the trail from Zermatt to Furi. You can rent poles in the village from shops like Bayard Sport. You have to wear comfortable walking shoes and dress in layers. This low-impact exercise is great for all ages and fitness levels. Rentals cost around CHF 15 per day, and the trails are open from dawn to dusk.

CHAPTER 10
ST. MORITZ

The town is about 1,800 meters above sea level, giving you stunning views of mountains and lakes. It became famous as a winter sports destination in the late 1800s when Johannes Badrutt invited his guests to enjoy the winter here. This started winter tourism.

When you walk around St. Moritz, you see a mix of old charm and modern luxury. The grand hotels, like Badrutt's Palace and the Kulm Hotel, have hosted royalty and celebrities for over a hundred years. These hotels are beautiful and offer great views, showing the town's rich history and luxurious present.

For skiing and snowboarding, the Corviglia, Corvatsch, and Diavolezza ski areas are perfect. You can get to the slopes using the Gornergrat Railway or the Matterhorn Glacier Paradise cable car. The ski season runs from late November to early May, and you can even ski on the glacier in summer.

If you like hiking, the best time is from June to September. You can start hikes from the village or take a funicular to Sunnegga or a cable car to Gornergrat for higher trails. The Five Lakes Walk is popular, offering great views and reflections of the Matterhorn in clear lakes.

In winter, Lake St. Moritz hosts the White Turf horse races every February. This event has been around since 1907 and attracts visitors from all over. Another place to visit is the Segantini Museum, which shows the work of Giovanni Segantini, inspired by the local landscapes.

ATTRACTIONS

Lake St. Moritz

Lake St. Moritz is right in the heart of the town, making it very easy to access. In summer, the 4-kilometer path around the lake is perfect for walking or biking, offering beautiful views and fresh mountain air. You can rent bikes from shops in the town center. Water activities like kayaking and paddleboarding are popular on the clear, calm waters of the lake.

In winter, the lake freezes solid and hosts unique events such as the White Turf horse races and the Snow Polo World Cup, typically held in February. These events draw visitors from around the world. To get there, just take a short walk from the town center. The lake is always open and free to visit, but check local schedules for event dates if you're interested in the winter activities. The frozen lake provides a picturesque backdrop for photos, so don't forget your camera. These winter events have been traditions for over a century, reflecting the town's long-standing reputation as a premier winter sports destination.

Diavolezza

Diavolezza is a mountain area offering stunning views and exciting outdoor activities. You can reach it by taking a scenic train ride from St. Moritz to the Bernina Diavolezza station, which takes about 30 minutes. From there, a cable car ride to the top takes about 10 minutes, offering breathtaking views along the way. A round-trip ticket for the cable car costs around CHF 35.

In the winter, Diavolezza is awesome for skiing and snowboarding, with slopes suited for all levels. The ski season here typically runs from November to April. During summer, it's a hiker's paradise. The trails, which are best explored from June to September, provide panoramic views of the surrounding peaks and glaciers.

The area is open daily from 8 AM to 5 PM. At the top, you'll find the Diavolezza Berghaus, a restaurant where you can enjoy a meal while taking in the spectacular scenery. The name Diavolezza comes from local legends about a beautiful witch said to have lived in the mountains, adding a touch of mystery to the place.

Segantini Museum

The Segantini Museum, dedicated to the life and works of the renowned artist Giovanni Segantini, is located on Via Somplaz. It's about a 10-minute walk from the center of St. Moritz, making it easily accessible. The museum's building itself is a work of art, designed to reflect the spirit of Segantini's works.

The entrance fee is CHF 12 for adults. The museum is open from Tuesday to Sunday, from 10 AM to 6 PM, and it is closed on Mondays. Inside, you'll find an impressive collection of Segantini's paintings, which vividly capture the beauty of the Engadin valley and the alpine landscapes.

PLACES TO EAT

Restaurant Kulm Country Club

You'll find Restaurant Kulm Country Club in the historic Kulm Hotel at Via Veglia 18, just a short walk from the town center. Open daily from 12 PM to 10 PM, this charming and elegant place offers a delightful mix of local and international dishes. Main courses range from CHF 30 to CHF 70. You should definitely try their truffle dishes and freshly made pasta. For dessert, the apple strudel is a must. The large windows offer beautiful mountain views, making your meal even more special.

La Marmite

La Marmite is located at the top of Corviglia, one of the highest gourmet restaurants in Europe. To get there, take the Corviglia funicular from the town center, which itself is a scenic and enjoyable ride. The restaurant is open from 11 AM to 4 PM, making it perfect for a luxurious lunch after a morning of skiing or hiking. Dishes cost between CHF 40 and CHF 100. You must try their truffle pizza and caviar, which are famous specialties. The views from La Marmite are breathtaking, offering panoramic vistas of the snow-covered mountains.

Chesa Veglia

Chesa Veglia, one of the oldest farmhouses in the area, has been converted into a delightful restaurant at Via Veglia 2, near the Kulm Hotel. This cozy spot offers three different dining areas, each with its unique menu. It's open daily from 6 PM to 11 PM. Main courses range from CHF 25 to CHF 60. Here, you can enjoy traditional Swiss dishes like raclette and fondue, prepared to perfection. Their wood-fired oven pizzas are also very popular and a must-try. The rustic decor and warm atmosphere make it a perfect place for a relaxed and hearty meal. Don't miss their homemade desserts, especially the chocolate fondant, which is a favorite among diners.

Badrutt's Palace Le Restaurant

Le Restaurant at Badrutt's Palace offers a fine dining experience focusing on French cuisine. Located at Via Serlas 27, just a short walk from the town center, this elegant restaurant is open from 7 PM to 11 PM and has a dress code that enhances the sophisticated atmosphere. Main courses are priced between CHF 50 and CHF 100. The menu features exquisite dishes like foie gras and lobster, along with a variety of gourmet French specialties. The extensive wine list offers selections from around the world, perfect for pairing with your meal. The dining room is beautifully decorated, creating a romantic and refined setting. For dessert, the crème brûlée is highly recommended for its creamy texture and rich flavor.

Hauser Restaurant

Hauser Restaurant is a beloved family-run establishment known for its cozy ambiance and delicious Swiss dishes. It's located at Via Traunter Plazzas 7, right in the heart of town, making it easily accessible. Open daily from 7 AM to 11 PM, it's a great spot for breakfast, lunch, or dinner. Prices for main courses range from CHF 20 to CHF 40. Be sure to try the Rösti, a traditional Swiss potato dish that's crispy and flavorful. Their homemade cakes and pastries are also a highlight, perfect for a sweet treat. The outdoor terrace is a lovely place to dine in the summer, offering a great view of the bustling town square.

Dal Mulin

Dal Mulin offers Mediterranean cuisine with a Swiss twist. Located at Via Maistra 33, it's a short walk from the main shopping area, making it a convenient dining option. The restaurant is open from Tuesday to Sunday, 6:30 PM to 10 PM. Main courses range from CHF 30 to CHF 70. The seafood dishes here are outstanding, particularly the grilled octopus and seafood risotto, prepared with fresh, high-quality ingredients. The wine selection is excellent, offering a variety of choices to complement your meal. The interior is modern and stylish, creating a relaxed yet elegant dining environment. For dessert, the panna cotta is a creamy and delicious way to end your meal.

Veltlinerkeller

For a traditional Engadine cuisine, visit Veltlinerkeller, is located at Via dal Bagn 11, close to the town center. The restaurant is open daily from 11:30 AM to 2 PM for lunch and 6 PM to 10 PM for dinner. Prices are moderate, with main courses costing between CHF 25 and CHF 50. Must-try dishes include the Capuns, a local specialty made with Swiss chard and dumplings, and the venison dishes in autumn, which are rich and flavorful. The restaurant has a rustic charm, with wooden interiors and a warm.

WHERE TO STAY

Badrutt's Palace Hotel

You'll find Badrutt's Palace Hotel right in the heart of town at Via Serlas 27. This luxury hotel has rooms starting at around CHF 600 per night, and the views of Lake St. Moritz and the surrounding mountains are breathtaking. The hotel offers several gourmet restaurants, a world-class spa, and a heated outdoor pool, so you can swim while taking in the stunning alpine scenery. It's a short walk from the train station, and if you prefer, the hotel provides a shuttle service. The service here is top-notch, and the atmosphere is both elegant and welcoming. It's perfect if you're looking to treat yourself to a luxurious stay with all the best amenities and personalized service.

Kulm Hotel St. Moritz

Kulm Hotel, located at Via Veglia 18, is another excellent luxury option, offering elegant rooms that start at about CHF 550 per night. This hotel combines its rich history with modern luxury. The amenities include a fantastic spa with various treatments, several gourmet restaurants offering a range of cuisines, and an indoor pool with stunning views of the mountains. It's an easy walk from the town center, and if you're arriving by train, a quick taxi ride will get you there in minutes. Staying at the Kulm Hotel feels like stepping into a world of elegance and history, where every detail is designed to provide comfort and sophistication.

Hotel Nolda

For a more budget-friendly option, consider Hotel Nolda at Via Crasta 3. This charming hotel is conveniently located near the Signalbahn cable car, making it an excellent base for skiing and exploring the area. The cozy rooms start at about CHF 150 per night, offering great value for the price. The hotel provides free Wi-Fi, a restaurant serving delicious local dishes, and a bar where you can relax after a day on the slopes. It's about a 15-minute walk from the town center, or you can take a local bus if you prefer.

Hauser Swiss Quality Hotel

Hauser Swiss Quality Hotel is a fantastic mid-range option located at Via Traunter Plazzas 7, right in the bustling town center. The modern and comfortable rooms start from CHF 200 per night, making it an excellent choice for travelers looking for quality and convenience. The hotel is famous for its in-house restaurant, which serves delicious homemade pastries, and a rooftop terrace that offers stunning views of the town and surrounding mountains. It's easily accessible from the train station with just a short walk. This hotel is perfect if you want to be in the heart of the action, with shops, restaurants, and attractions right at your doorstep. **Hotel Steffani**

Hotel Steffani, another great mid-range option, is located at Via Traunter Plazzas 6, also in the central part of town. The stylish rooms start around CHF 250 per night and offer a range of amenities including a spa, indoor pool, and three different restaurants. The central location means you're just steps away from all the local attractions and the train station. The variety of amenities and the comfortable, stylish rooms make it a great choice for travelers who want a bit more comfort and convenience without the high price tag of a luxury hotel.

Youth Hostel St. Moritz

If you're traveling on a tight budget, Youth Hostel St. Moritz at Via Surpunt 60 offers an excellent option. Dormitory beds start at CHF 50 per night, and private rooms are available if you prefer more privacy. The hostel provides a free breakfast, Wi-Fi, and a communal kitchen, which is great for saving on food costs. It's located a bit farther from the town center, about a 25-minute walk, but there are regular buses that make it easy to get around. This hostel is perfect if you're looking to save money and meet other travelers.

WINTER SPORTS

Skiing and Snowboarding

You're going to love skiing and snowboarding here. The main ski areas are Corviglia, Corvatsch, and Diavolezza. To get to Corviglia, take the funicular from the town center. It's a quick and scenic ride. Corvatsch and Diavolezza are also easy to get to by bus or taxi from town. A day pass usually costs around CHF 80 to CHF 100.

Once you're on the slopes, you'll find runs for every skill level. If you're a beginner, you can take lessons with friendly instructors who will help you get started or improve your skills. For advanced skiers and snowboarders, there are plenty of challenging trails to enjoy. The resorts have everything you need, including rental shops for gear, cozy mountain huts where you can warm up with hot drinks and snacks, and panoramic restaurants where you can take in the stunning views while you eat. Always wear a helmet and check the weather and snow conditions before you go. The best time to ski is in the morning when the slopes are freshly groomed.

Ice Skating

For some fun ice skating, head to the Kulm Country Club Ice Rink or the Ludains Ice Arena. Both are close to the town center, so you can easily walk or take a short taxi ride. Entry costs around CHF 10 to CHF 15, and you can rent skates if you don't have your own.

These rinks are great for all skill levels. Whether you're just starting out or you've been skating for years, you'll have a great time. You can also catch ice hockey matches or figure skating performances if you prefer to watch. Wear warm, comfortable clothes that allow you to move easily, and make sure your skates fit properly to avoid blisters.

Snowshoeing and Winter Hiking

Snowshoeing and winter hiking are fantastic ways to explore the beautiful winter landscapes at a more relaxed pace. Popular trails are near Lake St. Moritz and in the Engadine Valley. You can start your adventure right from town or take a bus to one of the trailheads. Most trails are free to use, but if you want a guided experience, expect to pay around CHF 50 to CHF 100 per person.

These trails are well-marked and range from easy to challenging, so you can find one that suits your fitness level. Snowshoeing lets you walk over the snow without sinking, making it easier to enjoy the scenery.

Bobsledding

For a real adrenaline rush, try bobsledding at the Olympia Bob Run, the oldest bobsleigh track in the world. It's a short drive from town, and you can easily get there by taxi or bus. A ride on the bobsled can be quite pricey, costing around CHF 250 to CHF 300 per person, but the experience is truly unforgettable.

You'll ride with professional drivers and brakemen who ensure your safety while you zoom down the icy track at thrilling speeds. The ride offers an exhilarating rush and a unique way to experience St. Moritz's winter sports heritage. Wear warm, snug clothing and secure footwear. Listen carefully to the safety instructions given by the professionals. I can assure that this activity is intense but incredibly exciting.

Cross-Country Skiing

If you prefer cross-country skiing, the Engadine Valley offers over 200 kilometers of well-groomed trails. These trails are accessible from various points around St. Moritz and can be reached by local buses or a short drive. While many trails are free, renting equipment will cost around CHF 20 to CHF 40 per day.

Even if you are a beginner or an experienced skier, you'll find trails that suit your level. Enjoy the tranquility and beauty of the winter landscape as you glide along these scenic paths. Guided tours and lessons are also available if you want to learn more about the sport and improve your skills. Dress in layers to manage your body temperature, and ensure your equipment is well-fitted and in good condition.

Ice Climbing

For a unique and challenging adventure, try ice climbing on the frozen waterfalls and ice structures around the Engadine Valley. These climbing spots are accessible by car or bus, with some requiring a short hike to reach the starting point. Guided ice climbing sessions cost around CHF 150 to CHF 300 per person, including equipment rental.

CHAPTER 11
LUGANO

Lugano is a beautiful city in the Italian-speaking part of Switzerland. **It's right on the northern shore of Lake Lugano, surrounded by the Swiss Alps.** This city has a nice history too going back to Roman times, with Italian influences.

When you walk through the town center, **you'll see narrow cobblestone streets, charming piazzas, and beautiful churches.** Check out the Cattedrale di San Lorenzo; it's got stunning architecture and amazing frescoes that give you a peek into the past. The streets are full of cozy cafes and shops where you can relax and enjoy the place.

The lake is one of the best parts. Try to Imagine on a boat ride, taking in the calm water and the mountains around you. If you stay on land, the lakefront promenade is perfect for a walk. You'll find benches along the way where you can sit and enjoy the view. If you like water sports, try paddleboarding or kayaking.

The parks and gardens are lovely too. **Parco Ciani is the biggest park in the city, right by the lake.**

There's always something happening here. **The city hosts several festivals and events throughout the year.** The Lugano Festival is great for classical music lovers, and Estival Jazz is a great open-air jazz festival. The LAC Lugano Arte e Cultura is a modern cultural center where you can catch concerts and theater performances.

Shopping is a treat. **Via Nassa is the main shopping street with high-end boutiques, local shops, and Swiss watchmakers.** Don't miss the local markets for fresh produce, local cheeses, and handmade crafts. Is also the perfect place to find souvenirs.

Food is a highlight. **The cuisine here is full of Italian flavors.** Think of delicious pasta, risotto, and seafood at great restaurants. Try local dishes like polenta and braised beef. And you can't leave without having some gelato, perfect for enjoying while you walk along the lake. I suggest!

ATTRACTIONS

Lake Lugano is right in the center of the city. To get the full experience, take a boat ride from the Lugano Paradiso dock. Boats run often, and you can check times online or at the dock. For a relaxing walk, follow the lakefront path. Benches are placed along the way for sitting and enjoying the view. Morning and late afternoon are the best times for photos. You can rent paddleboards and kayaks at several spots along the shore if you enjoy water sports.

Parco Ciani is the largest park in Lugano, located at the end of the lakefront promenade. The park is open all year and free to enter. It's full of greenery, tall trees, and colorful flowers. The well-maintained paths make it easy to explore. You can have a picnic on the grassy areas or relax by the many sculptures and fountains. Spring and summer are the best times to visit, as the gardens are in full bloom, creating a colorful and serene environment.

Monte Brè offers amazing views of Lugano, Lake Lugano, and the Alps.

To get there, take the funicular from the Cassarate station in Lugano. The funicular runs every 30 minutes, and you can buy tickets at the station. The ride takes about 10 minutes, offering spectacular views as you go up. Once at the top, there are hiking trails for all levels. You'll also find restaurants at the summit where you can enjoy a meal with a breathtaking view. It's perfect for nature lovers and those seeking outdoor activities.

LAC Lugano Arte e Cultura is located near the lakefront at Piazza Bernardino Luini 6. It's the cultural hub of the city, hosting concerts, theater performances, and art exhibitions. The building itself is an architectural marvel. Check their website for the schedule of events during your visit. The center is open Tuesday to Sunday from 10 AM to 6 PM. You can enjoy contemporary art exhibits or live performances in this dynamic space.

Gandria is a charming village about 4 kilometers from the city center. You can reach Gandria by boat or bus. Boats depart regularly from Lugano, and the journey takes about 30 minutes, offering beautiful views along the way. Alternatively, you can take a bus from the main station. Once in Gandria, explore the narrow streets, stone houses, and picturesque views. Enjoy the peaceful atmosphere, have lunch at a local restaurant, and take in the stunning lake views. It's a perfect day trip that gives you a taste of traditional Swiss-Italian village life.

Swissminiatur is a miniature park located in Melide, about 8 kilometers from Lugano. Take a quick train ride from Lugano's main station to Melide station, which takes about 10 minutes. The park is open from mid-March to late October, from 9 AM to 6 PM. It features detailed miniatures of famous Swiss buildings and landscapes. It's fun and educational, especially if you're traveling with children. There is an entrance fee, but it's worth it to see the intricate models and learn about Swiss landmarks. You can easily spend a few hours here, marveling at the miniatures and enjoying the park's setting.

PLACES TO EAT

Ristorante Galleria Arté al Lago is located at Via Cattori 4 and is part of the Grand Hotel Villa Castagnola. To get here, take a bus to the Castagnola stop and walk a short distance. This Michelin-starred restaurant offers stunning views of Lake Lugano, creating a perfect dining atmosphere. Specializing in creative seafood dishes, you can expect to pay around CHF 150 per person for a full meal, but it's well worth the price for the quality and presentation. The restaurant is open Tuesday to Saturday for lunch from 12 PM to 2 PM and for dinner from 7 PM to 10 PM. Make sure to try their signature seafood platter, which showcases a variety of fresh seafood prepared with exquisite finesse. For dessert, the chocolate fondant is a must-try, offering a rich, melt-in-your-mouth experience that perfectly rounds off your meal.

Ristorante La Cucina di Alice can be found at Riva Paradiso 36, just a short walk from the Lugano Paradiso funicular station. The cozy and inviting atmosphere makes it a perfect spot for a relaxing meal. The menu focuses on fresh, local ingredients, with dishes crafted to highlight regional flavors. Main dishes range from CHF 25 to CHF 50, making it an affordable option for high-quality dining. The restaurant is open every day from 12 PM to 2:30 PM and 7 PM to 10:30 PM. You should definitely try the risotto with local saffron, which is creamy, flavorful, and truly memorable. For dessert, the tiramisu is light and airy, offering a sweet end to your meal.

Antica Osteria del Porto is situated at Via Foce 9, near the lake, providing a beautiful setting for your dining experience. You can get here by taking a bus to the Foce stop and walking a few minutes. The rustic and welcoming ambiance makes it a popular spot for both locals and tourists. The menu features traditional Ticinese cuisine, with main courses priced between CHF 20 and CHF 40. The restaurant is open Monday to Saturday from 12 PM to 2 PM and 6:30 PM to 10 PM. Be sure to order the polenta with braised beef, a hearty dish that's rich in flavor. For dessert, the homemade chestnut cake is a perfect choice, offering a sweet and nutty taste that's simply delicious.

Grotto Morchino is located at Via Morchino 4 in Pambio-Noranco. This grotto is a bit off the beaten path but definitely worth the visit. Take a bus to the Pambio-Noranco stop and walk a short distance to reach the restaurant. The cozy and authentic atmosphere makes you feel like you've stepped into a local's home. The restaurant specializes in hearty Ticinese dishes, with mains ranging from CHF 25 to CHF 50. They are open Tuesday to Sunday from 12 PM to 2:30 PM and 7 PM to 11 PM. Don't miss the rabbit stew, which is tender and full of flavor. For dessert, their panna cotta is creamy and delicious, making it a perfect way to end your meal. The outdoor seating area is particularly charming during the warmer months, surrounded by greenery and offering a peaceful dining experience.

Ristorante Al Portone is located at Via Pioda 8, close to the city center, making it easily accessible by foot from the main shopping streets. The elegant setting of the restaurant makes it perfect for a special night out. The menu offers a mix of Mediterranean and local dishes, with main courses priced between CHF 30 and CHF 60. The restaurant is open Monday to Saturday from 12 PM to 2 PM and 7 PM to 10:30 PM. The lamb chops are highly recommended; they are tender, juicy, and cooked to perfection. For dessert, try the lemon sorbet, which is refreshing and the perfect palate cleanser. The restaurant also boasts an excellent wine selection.

WHERE TO STAY

Hotel Splendide Royal Located on Riva Antonio Caccia 7, this luxurious hotel sits right by Lake Lugano, offering stunning views and elegant accommodations. To get here, you can take a bus to the Tassino stop and walk a short distance. The hotel provides a range of services, including a spa, fitness center, and gourmet restaurant. Rooms start at around CHF 350 per night, offering a truly indulgent experience. The hotel is open 24 hours, so you can check in whenever you arrive. The staff are known for their exceptional service, ensuring your stay is as comfortable and memorable as possible. Imagine waking up to a breathtaking view of the lake from your room and starting your day with a leisurely stroll along the lakefront promenade.

Villa Sassa Hotel, Residence & Spa Situated at Via Tesserete 10, this hotel is nestled in a lush garden setting, offering a peaceful retreat while still being close to the city center. You can reach it by taking a bus to the Besso stop and walking a short distance. The hotel features spacious rooms, a full-service spa, and an outdoor pool. Prices start at around CHF 200 per night, providing good value for a luxurious stay. Open 24 hours, the hotel offers a relaxing atmosphere with top-notch amenities. Enjoy the panoramic views of Lugano from the terrace and unwind in the spa after a day of exploring the city.

Hotel Federale Located at Via Paolo Regazzoni 8, this mid-range hotel is just a short walk from the Lugano main train station, making it incredibly convenient for travelers. The hotel offers comfortable rooms and friendly service, with prices starting at around CHF 150 per night. It is open 24 hours, which is perfect for those who need easy access to transportation. The hotel provides a breakfast buffet and has a small fitness area, making it a great option if you want convenience and good value. Visit the nearby shops and restaurants, all within walking distance from the hotel.

Lugano Dante Center Swiss Quality Hotel Found at Piazza Cioccaro 5, this centrally located hotel is ideal for those who want to be in the heart of the action. You can easily reach it by taking the funicular from the Lugano train station to the city center. Rooms start at around CHF 200 per night, offering modern amenities and exceptional service. The hotel is open 24 hours, providing a comfortable and convenient stay. They offer a complimentary breakfast and have a cozy bar area where you can relax. This hotel is a fantastic choice if you want to visit the city's attractions and nightlife, with everything right outside your doorstep.

Youth Hostel Lugano Savosa Located at Via Cantonale 13 in Savosa, a suburb of Lugano, this budget-friendly option is perfect for backpackers and young travelers. You can reach it by taking a bus to the Savosa stop and walking a short distance. Dormitory beds start at around CHF 35 per night, with private rooms available for a bit more. The hostel is open from 7 AM to 10 PM, offering basic amenities like free Wi-Fi, a communal kitchen, and a garden area. It's a great place to meet fellow travelers and enjoy a social atmosphere. Take advantage of the nearby hiking trails and local cafes.

Hotel City Lugano Located at Via Giuseppe Bagutti 4, close to the University of Lugano. You can reach it by taking a bus to the Università stop and walking a short distance. This modern hotel offers sleek, contemporary rooms starting at around CHF 180 per night. Open 24 hours, it provides amenities such as free Wi-

Fi, a fitness center, and a breakfast buffet. It's an excellent choice for business travelers and those who prefer a modern, stylish environment.

Grand Hotel Villa Castagnola Located at Viale Castagnola 31, this historic hotel is set in a subtropical park, offering a luxurious and tranquil stay. To get here, take a bus to the Castagnola stop and walk a short distance. Rooms start at around CHF 400 per night, reflecting its status as a top-tier accommodation option. Open 24 hours, the hotel features an indoor pool, spa, and fine dining options. It's perfect for those seeking elegance and relaxation.

DAY TRIPS

Gandria

Gandria is a charming village located just 5 kilometers east of the city on the shores of Lake Lugano. To get there, take a scenic boat ride from the main pier, which takes about 30 minutes, or catch a bus to the Gandria stop. Once you arrive, you'll find narrow, winding streets filled with picturesque stone houses and flower-filled balconies. Start your day with a visit to the **Museum of Swiss Customs**, which provides fascinating insights into local history and culture. The museum is open from 10 AM to 5 PM, and the entry fee is CHF 5. After exploring the museum, enjoy a leisurely lunch at one of the lakeside restaurants, such as **Ristorante Antico**, where you can try local Ticinese dishes like polenta and braised beef. Spend the afternoon strolling along the Olive Trail, a scenic path that offers breathtaking views of the lake and the surrounding mountains. This trail takes about an hour to walk and is suitable for all fitness levels.

Bellinzona

Bellinzona, the capital of the Canton of Ticino, is about 30 kilometers north of the city. You can easily reach it by train in just 20 minutes from the main station. Bellinzona is famous for its three medieval castles, which are UNESCO World Heritage sites. Start your visit at **Castelgrande**, located right in the city center. The castle is open from 10 AM to 5 PM, and entry costs CHF 5. Explore the ancient towers and ramparts, and enjoy panoramic views of the city. Next, take a short walk to **Montebello Castle**, which offers more historical exhibits and stunning views. Finally, visit **Sasso Corbaro Castle**, the highest of the three, for its unique architecture and beautiful gardens. For lunch, head to **Ristorante Grotto dei Pini**, where you can enjoy traditional dishes like risotto and Ticinese sausages. In the afternoon, wander through Bellinzona's old town, with its charming streets, historic buildings, and lively markets.

Lake Como

Lake Como, just across the border in Italy, is about 30 kilometers away and easily accessible by train or car. A train ride to Como city takes about 30 minutes. Start your day with a visit to the beautiful **Cathedral of Como**, which is open from 7:30 AM to 7 PM and free to enter. Then, take the funicular up to Brunate, a small village with stunning views of the lake and surrounding mountains. The funicular operates from 8 AM to 10:30 PM, and a round-trip ticket costs CHF 5. Enjoy a leisurely lunch at **Ristorante Bellavista**, which offers delicious Italian cuisine with panoramic views. In the afternoon, take a boat tour of Lake Como, which departs regularly from the Como pier and costs around CHF 15. The boat ride allows you to see the elegant villas and gardens that line the lake. End your day with a relaxing stroll along the lakefront promenade before heading back.

Morcote

Morcote, a picturesque village on the shores of Lake Lugano, is about 10 kilometers away. You can reach it by boat, which takes about 45 minutes, or by bus. Morcote is known for its beautiful gardens and historic architecture. Start your visit at the **Scherrer Park**, a stunning botanical garden with a mix of Mediterranean and subtropical plants, sculptures, and architectural elements from different cultures. The park is open from 10 AM to 6 PM, and entry costs CHF 8. Next, visit the **Church of Santa Maria del Sasso**, an ancient church with beautiful frescoes and a commanding view of the lake. For lunch, dine at **Ristorante della Torre**, where you can enjoy local specialties like fish from the lake. In the afternoon, take a leisurely walk through the village's narrow streets, lined with charming houses and artisan shops. The peaceful atmosphere and beautiful scenery make Morcote a perfect day trip destination.

FoxTown Factory Stores

If you love shopping, a visit to FoxTown Factory Stores in Mendrisio is a must. Located about 15 kilometers south, you can reach FoxTown by train in just 20 minutes. The outlet mall is open daily from 11 AM to 7 PM and offers a wide range of discounted luxury brands. Spend the day browsing through over 160 stores, including famous brands like Gucci, Prada, and Versace, offering discounts of up to 70%. For lunch, there are several restaurants and cafes within the mall where you can take a break and enjoy a meal. After a full day of shopping, relax with a coffee before heading back with your bags full of bargains.

SCENIC TRAIN RIDES

T he Glacier Express, often referred to as the slowest express train in the world, is designed for you to fully appreciate the incredible scenery at a leisurely pace.

This train ride takes you from Zermatt to St. Moritz, covering approximately 290 kilometers over about 8 hours, providing you with panoramic views of mountains, valleys, and picturesque villages. When you start your visiting in Zermatt, you'll be greeted by views of the iconic Matterhorn. The train station is conveniently located in the town center, making it easy to start your adventure. As the train climbs to the Oberalp Pass, at 2,033 meters above sea level, you'll be treated to breathtaking views of snow-capped peaks and alpine meadows. This pass is particularly stunning in winter when everything is covered in a blanket of snow, creating a magical winter wonderland.

The Glacier Express takes you through the Rhine Gorge, often called the "Swiss Grand Canyon," featuring dramatic cliffs and winding rivers that offer some of the most awe-inspiring scenery along the route. One of the most iconic spots on this journey is the Landwasser Viaduct. This engineering marvel stands 65 meters high with six arches that curve into a tunnel in the cliff, making it one of the most photographed spots along the route. You have to book your tickets in advance, especially during peak travel seasons like summer and winter. Consider the Excellence Class for a good comfort and a gourmet meal served at your seat. I suggest you to take the window seat to get the best views throughout the trip. The best times to travel are in summer when you can enjoy lush green valleys and clear skies, and in winter when the snow-covered landscapes create a magical setting.

Bernina Express

The Bernina Express offers a breathtaking journey from Chur, Switzerland, to Tirano, Italy, blending alpine and Mediterranean scenery in a spectacular 4-hour ride. The trip begins with the Albula Line, featuring spiral tunnels and soaring bridges, and is a UNESCO World Heritage site showcasing impressive engineering feats. As the train ascends to the Bernina Pass at 2,253 meters, you'll be greeted with stunning views of glaciers and mountain peaks, with the clear alpine air enhancing the breathtaking scenery. Lago Bianco, a serene lake appearing milky white due to the glacial waters, offers a stark yet beautiful contrast to the rugged terrain surrounding it. The experience also takes you through the charming town of Poschiavo, where you can experience Italian culture and architecture through its narrow streets and traditional houses.

Visiting with Bernina Express, reserve your seats early, particularly in the panoramic carriages that feature large windows for unobstructed views. Tickets can be booked online or at major train stations. Bringing snacks and drinks is advisable, or you can purchase them on board. The best times to travel on the Bernina Express are during spring and autumn, when you can see the mild weather and fewer crowds, and in winter when the snowy landscapes and frozen lakes create a magical atmosphere.

GoldenPass Line

The GoldenPass Line connects Lucerne with Montreux, passing through beautiful Swiss countryside and charming towns over a 5-hour journey, with train changes at Interlaken and Zweisimmen. As the train passes by Lake Brienz, you'll see the turquoise waters and the Giessbach Falls. In Interlaken, nestled between Lake Thun and Lake Brienz, you'll see the lake and mountain views, making it a great spot for a quick stop to explore local attractions. Gstaad, a glamorous resort town, is known for its hotels and boutiques, offering a perfect blend of charm and elegance. Finally, the experience ends in Montreux, located on the shores of Lake Geneva, famous for its jazz festival and beautiful lakeside promenade lined with palm trees, perfect for a relaxing walk after your long day.

SWISS FESTIVALS AND EVENTS

Arrive in Basel early in the morning when it's still dark, and suddenly, at 4:00 AM, the entire city lights up with lanterns. This is how the Basel Carnival starts, right after Ash Wednesday. For 72 hours, you will see amazing parades with people wearing bright masks and costumes. The music is loud and fun, coming from bands called Guggenmusik. You can also enjoy special carnival foods like Mehlsuppe, which is a type of soup, and Zwiebelwähe, an onion tart. It's an event full of energy and tradition, perfect for experiencing Basel's unique culture. You can walk through the city and join the festivities.

Now, Lake Geneva in early July for the **Montreux Jazz Festival**.

For two weeks, Montreux becomes a music lover's paradise. You'll hear not just jazz, but all kinds of music from famous artists and new talents. You can move from one concert to another, enjoying different performances. There are also workshops and jam sessions where you can get closer to the music. The food stalls offer a international cuisines. Walking along the lake with live music in the background will be a great idea.

In early August, head to Zurich for the Street Parade. Over a million people dancing along Lake Zurich to electronic music. The floats, called Love Mobiles, have DJs playing live music, and the energy is incredible. You'll see nice costumes and lights, creating a huge party atmosphere. The parade is an all-day event with music, food stalls, and bars. It's like a giant open-air rave where everyone is enjoying the event.

When December comes, visit Geneva's Old Town for the **Fête de l'Escalade**. This festival celebrates a historic victory from 1602. Walking through narrow streets lit by torches, hearing musket fire, and seeing people in old costumes. The atmosphere is filled with history, and you can taste traditional vegetable soup and buy chocolate cauldrons filled with marzipan vegetables. The whole city joins in, making it a lively and historical celebration.

In early August, make your way to Locarno for the Locarno Film Festival. Watching international films under the stars at Piazza Grande, a big open-air theater. Over several days, you'll see world premieres and meet filmmakers. The setting is magical, with mountains around and warm summer air. It's perfect for movie lovers, and you'll get to enjoy films in a beautiful and perfect environment.

From late September to early October, experience Alpabzug, or the Descent from the Alps. Being in a Swiss village like Appenzell, seeing cows decorated with flowers and bells parading through the streets. This marks the end of summer when cattle come down from the mountains. Villages are alive with markets, music, and local food. It's a chance to see Swiss rural traditions up close. You can walk around, taste local specialties, and feel the festive atmosphere.

In November, visit Bern for Zibelemärit, the Onion Market. In the city center filled with stalls selling onions in every form. You'll see beautiful onion strings and smell onion tarts and soups. This festival is full of activity with crafts, music, and food, all dedicated to onions. Walking through the market, you can taste different onion dishes and buy unique onion-themed souvenirs.

If you plan far ahead, don't miss the Fête des Vignerons in Vevey, a festival that happens once every 20-25 years. Being on the shores of Lake Geneva, watching grand spectacles with thousands of performers. This festival celebrates the region's wine culture. You'll see big stage shows, hear music, and taste local wine. It's a rare event celebrating old traditions.

TRADITIONAL SWISS CUISINE

When you're traveling around and tasting the local food, it's one of the best ways to experience the culture with no jokes. You get a pot of melted cheese, usually a mix of Gruyère and Emmental, and you dip pieces of bread into it. It's warm and comforting, especially in the colder months. For an authentic experience, you should visit **Le Chalet de Gruyères** in Gruyères.

The atmosphere is cozy, and the **fondue** is incredible. Make sure to swirl your bread in a figure-eight motion to keep the cheese smooth.

Next, you have to try **raclette**. This involves heating cheese and scraping it off onto potatoes, pickles, and onions. It's simple but incredibly tasty. You should head to **Walliser Keller in Zurich** for a great raclette experience. They serve the cheese right at your table, and you can enjoy it with a variety of sides. Let the cheese get a bit crispy for extra flavor.

Another must-try is **Rösti**. This Swiss take on hash browns is made from grated potatoes fried until crispy. Sometimes it's served with bacon, onions, or even a fried egg on top. You should try it at **Zeughauskeller in Zurich**. Their Rösti is perfectly crispy and pairs well with their sausages.

For a sweet treat, you can't miss **Swiss chocolate**. The chocolate here is world-famous for a reason. Visit **Läderach** or **Sprüngli in Zurich** for some of the best chocolate you'll ever taste. Try their pralines and truffles, and don't forget to take some bars home as souvenirs.

In the German-speaking part of the country, you have to try **Zürcher Geschnetzeltes**. This dish is sliced veal in a creamy white wine and mushroom sauce, often served with Rösti. You can find an excellent version at **Kronenhalle in Zurich**. The restaurant itself is a piece of art, with works from famous artists like Picasso and Miró adorning the walls.

In the Italian-speaking region, try **Risotto**. Swiss risotto is creamy and often made with local ingredients like saffron. **Grotto della Salute in Lugano** serves a fantastic saffron risotto that's rich and flavorful.

Don't forget to try **Älplermagronen**, which is Swiss mac and cheese made with potatoes, macaroni, cheese, and topped with fried onions and applesauce. **Restaurant Swiss Chuchi in Zurich's old town** is the place to go for this dish.

SWISS CHOCOLATE AND CHEESE TOURS

Maison Cailler Chocolate Factory Tour in Broc is a must for any chocolate lover. **Cailler** is one of the oldest chocolate brands, founded in 1819 by François-Louis Cailler. At the factory, you'll start by learning about the history of chocolate and see how it's made from the cocoa bean to the delicious end product. Walk through interactive displays and watch chocolatiers at work. The highlight is tasting freshly made chocolates at the end. Book tickets online, especially during busy tourist seasons. The factory is near the Broc-Fabrique train station, which makes it easy to get to by public transport.

If you love Lindt chocolate, visit the **Lindt Home of Chocolate in Zurich**. Lindt was founded in 1845 and is famous for its smooth and creamy chocolate. See the world's largest chocolate fountain and learn about the entire chocolate-making process, from cocoa plantations to the final product. Taste various Lindt chocolates and visit their large chocolate shop. You can book tickets online. To get there, take a train to Kilchberg and then a short bus ride to the factory.

If you love cheese, the **Maison du Gruyère in Gruyères** offers a great tour. Gruyère cheese has been made in this region since the 12th century. See how Gruyère cheese is made through large viewing windows. Use an audio guide available in many languages to learn about the process. Enjoy a tasting session at the end. Book your tour on their website. The dairy is next to the Gruyères train station, making it easy to reach.

Another great cheese tour is at the **Emmental Show Dairy in Affoltern**. Emmental cheese, known for its characteristic holes, has been produced since the 13th century. Watch the traditional process of making Emmental cheese. The tour is interactive, and you can even try making cheese. Taste different varieties of Emmental cheese afterward. Book online and check the schedule for live demonstrations. The dairy is accessible by train and bus from Bern.

For a combined chocolate and cheese experience, take the **Chocolate Train from Montreux**. This scenic train ride goes through beautiful landscapes to both the Maison Cailler chocolate factory and the Maison du Gruyère cheese dairy. The train is a vintage Belle Epoque Pullman car. Enjoy guided tours of both factories with lots of tastings. Book tickets through the GoldenPass website. The train departs from Montreux, easily reachable by train from major cities.

HIKING AND NATURE TRAILS

The Eiger Trail is perfect if you want a bit of a challenge. This trail is about 6 kilometers long and is considered moderate in difficulty. You start at Eigergletscher Station and hike down to Alpiglen. Along the way, you get breathtaking views of the Eiger North Face. The Eiger is famous for its dramatic north face, first climbed in 1938. To reach the trail, take a train to Grindelwald and then the Jungfrau Railway to Eigergletscher Station. Wear sturdy hiking boots because some parts of the trail are rocky. The best time to hike here is from June to October when the weather is clear. There is no entry fee for the trail itself, but the train ride will cost around CHF 50-100 depending on your starting point.

The Five Lakes Walk (5-Seenweg) in Zermatt offers beautiful scenery without being too hard. This trail is around 10 kilometers long and takes you past five stunning lakes, each reflecting the mountains, including the famous Matterhorn. The hike is easy to moderate, suitable for most hikers, even families. Start at Blauherd, which you can reach by cable car from Zermatt. Zermatt has a rich history, with the Matterhorn first climbed in 1865. The best time to visit is from late June to early October. Here are some beautiful views, so you can take some photos too. The cable car ride costs around CHF 40-60, and the trail is free to hike.

The Schynige Platte to Faulhorn to First Trail is for those who love long hikes and want a challenge. It's about 16 kilometers long and is considered difficult, but the effort is worth it. You start at Schynige Platte and hike to Faulhorn, where you can see one of the oldest mountain hotels in the Alps, then continue to

First. This trail offers panoramic views of the Bernese Alps, including the Eiger, Mönch, and Jungfrau peaks. These peaks have a rich mountaineering history, with many climbs since the 19th century. The best months for this hike are July to September. To reach the trailhead, take a train to Wilderswil and then the Schynige Platte Railway. The train ride costs around CHF 30-70. The trail itself is free to access.

The Aletsch Glacier Panorama Trail offers some of the best glacier views in the Alps. This 13-kilometer trail is moderately difficult and takes you along the edge of the Aletsch Glacier, the largest glacier in the Alps. The glacier has been studied since the 19th century and is a UNESCO World Heritage Site. Start at the Bettmerhorn mountain station and hike to Fiescheralp. The trail is well-marked, but wear layers because the temperature can change. The best time to hike is from July to September. To get there, take a train to Betten and then a cable car to Bettmerhorn. The cable car ride costs around CHF 30-50. The trail itself is free to access.

For a family-friendly hike, the **Oeschinensee Lake Trail** near Kandersteg is perfect. This easy to moderate hike is around 8 kilometers long and leads you to the beautiful Oeschinen Lake. The lake has been a popular spot since the 19th century, known for its clear blue waters. Start from the Oeschinensee cable car station and follow the trail to the lake, where you can enjoy a picnic or swim in the summer. The trail is open from May to October. To reach the trailhead, take a train to Kandersteg and then a cable car to Oeschinensee. The cable car ride costs around CHF 20-30. There is no entry fee for the trail.

The Lavaux Vineyard Terraces Trail is great if you want a mix of hiking and wine tasting. This easy 11-kilometer trail winds through the terraced vineyards of Lavaux, a UNESCO World Heritage Site. The vineyards date back to the 11th century when monks began cultivating grapes. The trail stretches from St. Saphorin to Lutry, passing through charming villages with views of Lake Geneva and the Alps. Visit local wineries and sample the region's wines. The best time to hike is from April to October. To get there, take a train to St. Saphorin. The trail is free to access, but wine tastings typically cost CHF 10-20 per tasting.

SKI RESORTS AND WINTER ACTIVITIES

Zermatt is one of the best ski resorts, famous for its stunning views of the Matterhorn. The town of Zermatt has a rich history dating back to the early 19th century when it became a hub for mountaineers. Today, it offers a range of slopes for all levels, from beginners to advanced skiers. You start your journey by taking a train to Zermatt, as the town is car-free. From Zermatt, you can take the

Gornergrat Railway or one of the many cable cars to reach the slopes. **If you're new to skiing, there are plenty of ski schools in Zermatt that offer lessons. Equipment rental is straightforward, with many shops in the village providing skis, boots, and snowboards.** The best time to visit Zermatt is from December to April when the snow conditions are perfect. Besides skiing, you can enjoy winter hiking, ice skating, and even take a helicopter tour to see the mountains from above. **Prices for lift tickets range from CHF 75 to CHF 100 per day.**

St. Moritz is another top destination for winter sports, known for its luxury and glamour. This resort has hosted the Winter Olympics twice, so you know the skiing is world-class. St. Moritz's history dates back to 1864 when it became famous for winter tourism. There are over 350 kilometers of pistes, catering to all skill levels. **Beginners can take lessons from one of the many ski schools, and there are plenty of rental shops for equipment.** To get to St. Moritz, you can take a scenic train ride from Zurich or drive. **The best time to visit is from December to March.** Apart from skiing, St. Moritz offers activities like bobsledding, ice skating, and snowshoeing. Don't miss the famous Cresta Run, a natural ice skeleton track. **Lift tickets cost around CHF 85 to CHF 105 per day.**

Verbier is part of the 4 Vallées ski area and is known for its challenging slopes and vibrant après-ski scene. Verbier's history as a ski destination began in the 1920s. **If you're an advanced skier, you'll love the off-piste opportunities here. For beginners, there are gentle slopes and ski schools to get you started.** You can rent equipment in the village, and getting to Verbier is easy by train and cable car. **The best time to visit is from December to April.** Besides skiing, you can try paragliding, dog sledding, and snowshoeing. Verbier is also famous for its lively nightlife, with many bars and clubs to enjoy after a day on the slopes. **Lift tickets are priced between CHF 70 and CHF 90 per day.**

Davos-Klosters offers a great mix of slopes and is perfect for families. The resort has several ski areas, each with a variety of runs for all levels. **Beginners will find plenty of easy slopes and excellent ski schools.** Equipment rental shops are available in both Davos and Klosters. **The best time to visit is from December to April.** Apart from skiing, Davos-Klosters offers ice skating, snowboarding, and winter hiking. You can also ride the scenic Rhaetian Railway for some amazing views. **Lift tickets cost around CHF 60 to CHF 80 per day.**

Grindelwald is part of the Jungfrau region and offers breathtaking views of the Eiger, Mönch, and Jungfrau mountains. The resort has a range of slopes suitable for all levels. **Beginners can take lessons from local ski schools, and equipment rental is available in the village.** The best time to visit is from December to March. Besides skiing, Grindelwald offers activities like sledding, snowshoeing, and ice climbing. You can also take the Jungfrau Railway to the "Top of Europe" for stunning panoramic views. **Lift tickets range from CHF 65 to CHF 85 per day.**

For beginners, it's important to **take a lesson** from a qualified instructor, as this will help you learn the basics and stay safe on the slopes. Renting equipment instead of buying is a smart choice because you can try different types and find what suits you best. **Dress in layers** because the weather can change quickly in the mountains, and always wear a helmet to protect yourself from falls. Start on easy slopes, like green and blue runs, before moving on to more challenging terrain.

Equipment rental is straightforward at most resorts. **Intersport** and **Skiset** are two popular chains with rental shops in most ski resorts, offering a wide range of skis, snowboards, and boots. You can also find local shops at each resort, so check what's available and compare prices.

The **best time to visit** for skiing is from December to April, with Christmas and New Year being very popular, which means resorts can be crowded and prices higher. January and February offer the best snow and fewer crowds after the holiday season. March and April bring warmer weather, but the snow is still good, especially at higher altitudes.

PRACTICAL INFORMATION RECAP

Emergency Contacts

If you find yourself in an emergency, it's important to know the right numbers to call. Well, **For police assistance, dial 117. For medical emergencies, dial 144.** If there's a fire, call 118. **In a general emergency, dial 112**, which will connect you to the appropriate service. Additionally, keep the contact information for your country's embassy handy. **If you're from the United States, the embassy is in Bern, and you can reach them at +41 31 357 70 11.** Always carry a copy of your passport and insurance details. If you need medical care, the hospitals and clinics are excellent, so show your insurance information and ask for translation help if needed.

Local Customs and Traditions

Respecting local customs is important. **Be punctual for any appointments or social gatherings, as being on time is highly valued.** The locals appreciate cleanliness and order, so always dispose of your trash properly and keep noise levels down, especially in residential areas. When greeting someone, a firm handshake is standard, and for friends or acquaintances, three kisses on the cheek are common. **Avoid discussing controversial topics like politics and money, as the country is known for its neutrality and politeness.** Respect personal space, so avoid standing too close to others. If invited to someone's home, bring a small gift like flowers or chocolates. Always remove your shoes before entering a home unless the host insists otherwise. **Learning a few basic phrases in the local language (German, French, or Italian, depending on the region) can show respect and goodwill.**

Tipping Guidelines

Tipping is appreciated but not mandatory. **In restaurants, a service charge is usually included in the bill, but rounding up the amount or leaving a small tip for exceptional service is common.** For instance, if your bill is CHF 47, rounding it up to CHF 50 is fine. **In hotels, tipping porters CHF 1-2 per bag and leaving a small amount for housekeeping is appreciated.** For taxi drivers, rounding up the fare or adding a small tip is standard. When using other services like hairdressers or spa treatments, a tip of around 5-10% is appreciated. **Remember, tipping is always at your discretion and should reflect your satisfaction with the service.**

Shopping Tips and Souvenirs

Shopping here offers unique items to take home as souvenirs. **Popular items include Swiss chocolate, Swiss watches, Swiss Army knives, and Swiss cheese.** Visit well-known brands like Lindt for chocolate or local chocolatiers for unique selections. Swiss watches are a timeless gift, though they can be pricey. **For something traditional, consider a Swiss Army knife from Victorinox, known for high-quality knives.** Other souvenirs include cuckoo clocks and beautifully crafted music boxes. Many stores close early on Saturdays and are often closed on Sundays. **Non-EU residents can enjoy tax-free shopping, so ask for a tax-free shopping form in the store and present it at the airport to reclaim your VAT.** Bargaining isn't common, so prices are generally fixed. **At local markets, bring cash as not all vendors accept credit cards.** Enjoy shopping and look for these iconic items to bring a piece of your trip back home.

END

Thank you for using this guide to plan your trip to Switzerland. **I hope the information here helps you organize your travel day by day.** Things can change quickly, so please complement this guide with additional sources to stay updated.

It means a lot to me that you've trusted my guide. This is my first attempt at writing a travel guide, and your feedback will help me improve and keep it updated. **I've put my heart into this, hoping to inspire and assist you.**

Switzerland is a special place for me. I hope you enjoy its beauty, culture, and people as much as I do. **Have a wonderful journey, make unforgettable memories, and enjoy every moment.**

Safe travels, and enjoy your adventure in Switzerland. **Thank you again, and I can't wait to hear about your experiences.** Enjoy every step of your Swiss adventure!

Made in the USA
Las Vegas, NV
25 October 2024

10434508R00069